Sentence Analysis by Diagram

SENTENCE ANALYSIS BY DIAGRAM

A HANDBOOK FOR THE RAPID REVIEW OF ENGLISH SYNTAX

BY

HENRY C. EDGAR

INSTRUCTOR IN ENGLISH, THE HILL SCHOOL
POTTSTOWN, PA.

NEW YORK
NEWSON AND COMPANY

1611

TO THE TEACHER

DIAGRAMMING is rather widely opposed to-day simply because it used to be taught as an end in itself. But no device in the whole teaching of grammar proves more useful, if the teacher constantly bears in mind that it is only a means to another end. If the diagram method used is perfectly simple, transparent, and elastic, it will secure that moderate degree of uniformity necessary to the efficient teaching of classes, it will enable the pupil to visualize syntactical relations with extraordinary clearness, and in the analysis of sentences it will accomplish an enormous saving of time to both pupil and teacher.

Such a diagram method this Handbook ventures to offer, — a method so entirely simple as to be merely a shorthand mode of analysis: if the student understands a given construction, he will have no difficulty in diagramming it. As the fruit of practical experience this method is offered, in the certainty that it, or some system like it, is indispensable to really efficient teaching: but always on the strict condition that the teacher never allow diagramming to become a puzzle in itself, and that he seek to ascertain not so much whether the pupil understands diagramming as whether the pupil understands grammar.

The model sentences are intended primarily as a means of briefly reviewing all the commoner constructions of English grammar. With the aid of the Index, such a review may be conducted in any order. A review of these model sentences will prove highly useful in preparing classes for the study of rhetoric, or for the grammar questions in the college entrance examinations.

All disputed points of syntax and all impractical or purely philosophic distinctions have been avoided so far as possible; those that could not be avoided have been interpreted in the interests of simplicity, uniformity, efficiency — at times with little regard to historic or scientific grammar — in the belief that the American school child should be a precise speaker and writer, but hardly an accomplished philologist.

The nomenclature conforms to that of Buehler's *A Modern English Grammar Revised*, Newson and Company, New York, 1914, and incorporates, so far as has been done in that book, the terminology suggested by the *Report of the Joint Committee on Grammatical Nomenclature*, approved and recommended by the National Education Association and by the National Council of Teachers of English.

I wish to acknowledge my indebtedness to my colleagues in the English Department of The Hill School, for their large share in the origination and development of the methods presented in this Handbook, and for their many subsequent suggestions of great value.

H. C. E.

CONTENTS

INTRODUCTION

I

Mode of Study

The first step toward acquiring the ability to diagram sentences (and diagramming sentences means neither more nor less than explaining their grammatical structure) should be to study closely the construction illustrated in each of the model sentences, and the manner in which that construction is properly diagrammed; and not to proceed to the next model sentence until all the previous ones have been thoroughly mastered. The next step should be a great amount of practice in diagramming rather easy sentences of about twenty words in length — sentences like those in Exercise 1. After that, there should be ample practice with sentences like those in Exercise 2. The three other exercises, each of which is slightly harder than the one before it, are intended for advanced pupils.

II

Theory of the Diagram

The theory of the diagram system used in this book rests on three simple principles:

1. The main line of every clause should represent its subject, its verb, and its complement (if any).

2. All modifiers should be placed under what they modify.

3. The whole diagram should consist of unbroken straight lines, which represent the unbroken grammatical connection between all parts of the sentence; but an independent element should be unconnected in the diagram, because it is unconnected in grammar.

III

Abbreviations

Following is a list of the forms and constructions which should always be labeled; use the abbreviations indicated below:

Subject	S.
Verb	V.
Object complement (direct object)	O.C.
Retained object	Ret. O.
Subjective complement	S.C.
Objective complement	Obv. C.
Secondary object	Sec. O.
Indirect object	I.O.
Appositive	App.
Introductory word of a subordinate clause	Introd.
Infinitive (and Gerund)	Inf.
Participle	Part.

Vocative	Voc.
Exclamation	Excl.
Parenthetical expression	Parenth.
Pleonasm	Pleon.
Nominative Absolute	Nom. Abs.
Expletive	Expl.

Elliptical words supplied should be inclosed in parentheses.

A group of words used like a single word should be covered by a horizontal brace whenever clearness requires, as in the case of phrasal prepositions (see sentence 95), or of phrases or clauses used substantively (see sentences 27 and 38).

IV

Rules of Procedure

The following steps, in the order given, should always be taken, as the only sure and scientific mode of attacking a new sentence:

1. Read the sentence over till you understand it.
2. Supply all cases of ellipsis.
3. Pick out the finite verbs (*i.e.*, not infinitives or participles), and determine the subject or subjects of each; each separate set of verb and subject (either or both of which may be compound) is the heart of a separate clause.

4. Now that the separate clauses have been determined, pick out the subordinate clauses and lay them mentally aside; then put down the subject, verb, and complement (if any) of each main clause: this should be the first actual writing done.

5. Now add the other details in any order most convenient.

6. Never fail to ask the question, "Who, whom, or what?" after every verb-form, whether finite, infinitive, or participle; the answer will be the complement. If no answer is furnished by the sentence, there is no complement.

7. Make sure that you have not neglected to label all the forms and constructions in the sentence which are listed in Part III of this Introduction.

8. For greater safety, "prove" your diagram by reading the sentence from it, and noting any failures to correspond in wording or meaning with the written sentence before you.

9. Lastly, write above the diagram, *Simple*, *Compound*, *Complex*, or *Compound-complex*, as the case may require.

V

To Secure Clearness

Whenever the diagram method fails to make the construction of a word perfectly clear, label it plainly with an explanation of what you mean. Diagramming is not intended to be a puzzle in itself, but only a time-saving way of analyzing a sentence; and what your teacher wishes to know is not so much whether you understand diagramming as whether you understand grammar.

VI

To Secure Neatness

In order to secure neatness and legibility, turn your paper lengthwise if you are using theme paper, or take a double page for your diagram if you are using an examination book. Space your main clauses all the way from top to bottom, and the subject, verb, and complement of each main clause all the way from left to right; this will give you ample room for attaching numerous lengthy modifiers without overcrowding. If, however, you still lack space, continue the diagram elsewhere, indicating the unbroken grammatical connection by a number where you left off and the same number where you resume. This device should not be resorted to except when necessary. (For examples see sentences 45 and 95.)

VII

Function of Connectives

Words, phrases, or clauses, when joined by a coördinating conjunction, should be connected in the diagram by a vertical line, and on this line the conjunction should be written. (For examples see sentences 28, 34, and 48.)

A subordinate clause may be introduced by any one of five kinds of words — by a subordinating conjunction, a conjunctive adverb, an interrogative adverb, a relative pronoun, or an interrogative pronoun. A subordinating conjunction has only one use in the sentence, that of introducing a clause; it should accordingly be written first on the main line of its clause, and labeled *Introd.* to indicate that it is the introductory word. (For example see sentence 37.) The four other kinds of introductory words all serve two uses at once: they introduce a clause, and they also have some construction within the clause. They should accordingly be so placed in the diagram as to indicate this construction within the clause, and also labeled *Introd.* to indicate that they are introductory words. (For examples see sentences 35, 37, and 47.)

VIII

List of Connectives

Following is a list of the words more commonly used to connect or introduce clauses. The memorization of this list will go far towards enabling the student to distinguish main clauses from those that are dependent. Conjunctive adverbs are not easily distinguished from subordinating conjunctions: a conjunctive adverb, however, usually implies the idea of time or place.

Coördinating Conjunctions, which connect clauses of the same rank. (For example see sentence 34.)

also (= and)	or
and	so (= therefore)
but	still
for	therefore
hence (= therefore)	whereas
however (= nevertheless)	wherefore
nevertheless	while (= whereas)
nor	yet (= nevertheless)

Subordinating Conjunctions, which introduce subordinate clauses. (For example see sentence 37.)

although	so that
as (= because)	than
because	that (when not equivalent to *who*, *whom*, or *which*)
if	
lest	
provided (that)	though
since (= because)	

Conjunctive Adverbs, which introduce subordinate clauses. (For example see sentence 37.)

after	before
as (= while)	since (= after)

till	wherever
until	while (= during the time that)
when	whilst
whenever	why
where	

Interrogative Adverbs, which introduce subordinate clauses when they introduce indirect questions. (For example see sentence 47.)

if (= whether)	where
how	whether
when	why

Relative Pronouns, which introduce subordinate clauses. (For example see sentence 35.)

that (= who or which)	which
what	who

Interrogative Pronouns, which introduce subordinate clauses when they introduce indirect questions. (For example see sentence 47.)

what	who
which	

SENTENCE ANALYSIS BY DIAGRAM

MODEL SENTENCES

ILLUSTRATING THE COMMONER CONSTRUCTIONS OF ENGLISH GRAMMAR

1. **Nouns or Pronouns: subject and object complement.** [Buehler's *A Modern English Grammar Revised*, Newson and Co., §§ 21, 27, 39.]

I saw *John*.

SIMPLE SENTENCE

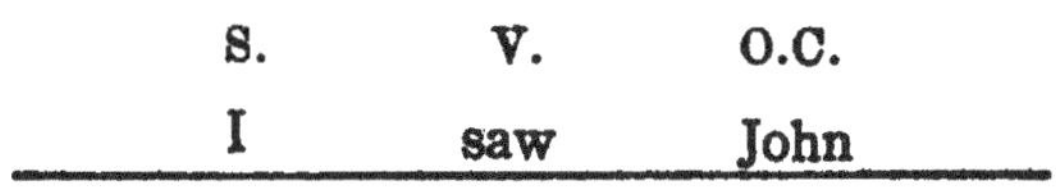

2. **Nouns or Pronouns: retained object.** [Buehler, § 188.]

I was handed a *chair*.

SIMPLE SENTENCE

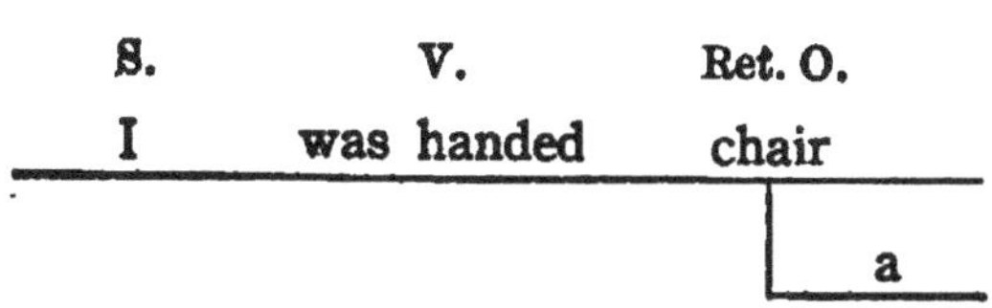

3. Nouns or Pronouns: subjective complement. [Buehler, § 38.]

I am *John.*

SIMPLE SENTENCE

S.	V.	S.C.
I	am	John

4. Nouns or Pronouns: objective complement. [Buehler, § 40.]

They elected Saul *king*.

SIMPLE SENTENCE

S.	V.	O.C.	Obv. C.
They	elected	Saul	King

5. Nouns or Pronouns: secondary object. [Buehler, § 53.]

I asked him *questions*.

SIMPLE SENTENCE

S.	V.	O.C.	Sec. O.
I	asked	him	questions

6. Nouns or Pronouns: indirect object. [Buehler, § 52.]

I told *him* the answers.

SIMPLE SENTENCE

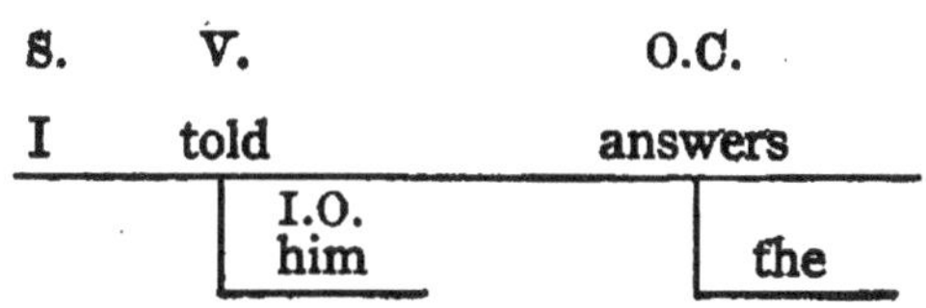

7. Nouns or Pronouns: possessive case. [Buehler, §§ 43 ff., 116, 133.]

Scott's novels were *his* delight.

SIMPLE SENTENCE

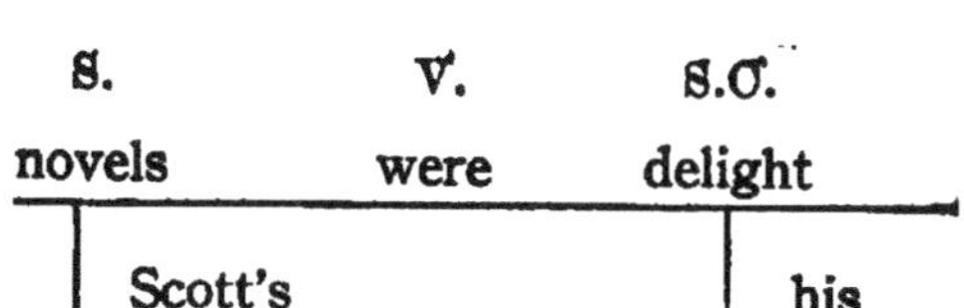

8. Nouns or Pronouns: appositive. [Buehler, § 54.]

He is John Doe, our ***captain.***

SIMPLE SENTENCE

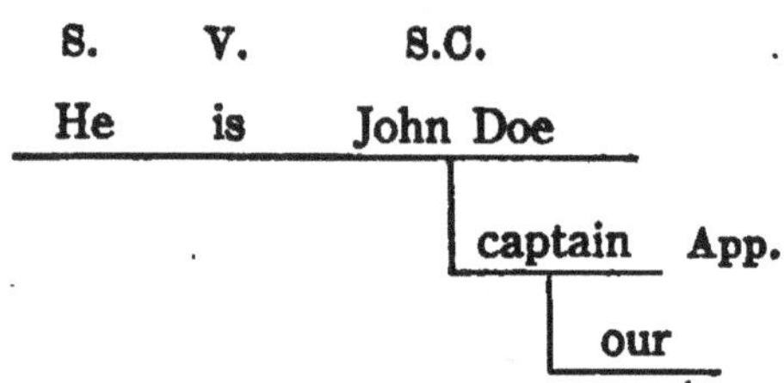

9. Nouns or Pronouns: object of a preposition. [Buehler, § 86.]

Mr. Smith of *New York* came to ***me.***

SIMPLE SENTENCE

10. Adjectives: modifier of a noun or pronoun. [Buehler, § 82.]

Good citizens are *honest* ones.

SIMPLE SENTENCE

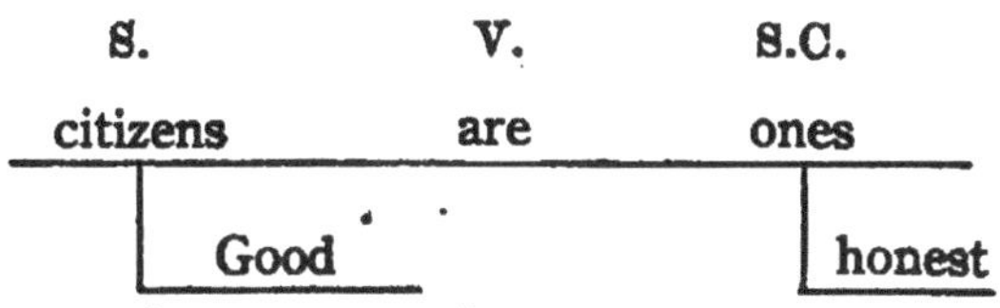

11. Adjectives: subjective complement. [Buehler, §§ 38, 167.]

Rattlesnakes are *venomous*.

SIMPLE SENTENCE

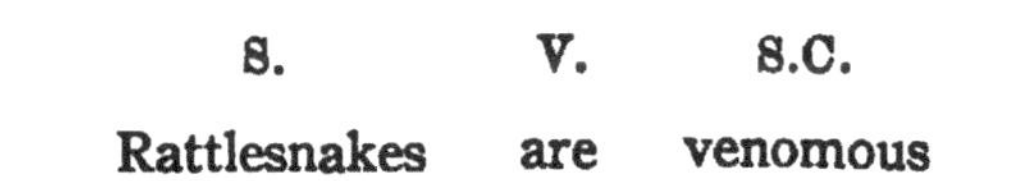

12. Adjectives: objective complement. [Buehler, § 40.]

I painted the house *green*.

SIMPLE SENTENCE

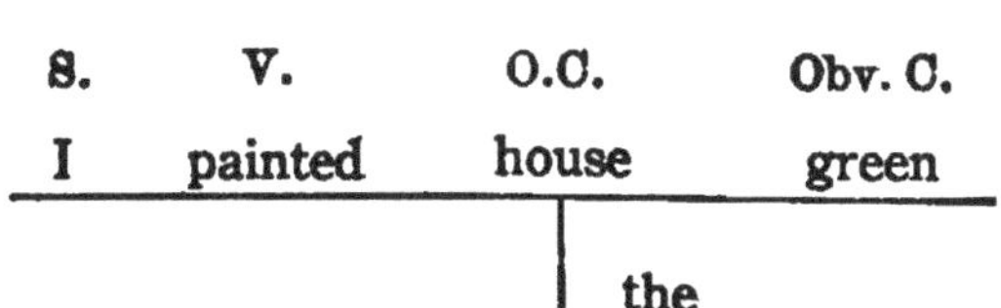

13. Adverbs: modifier of a verb. [Buehler, §§ 43 ff., 85.]

I ran *swiftly*.

SIMPLE SENTENCE

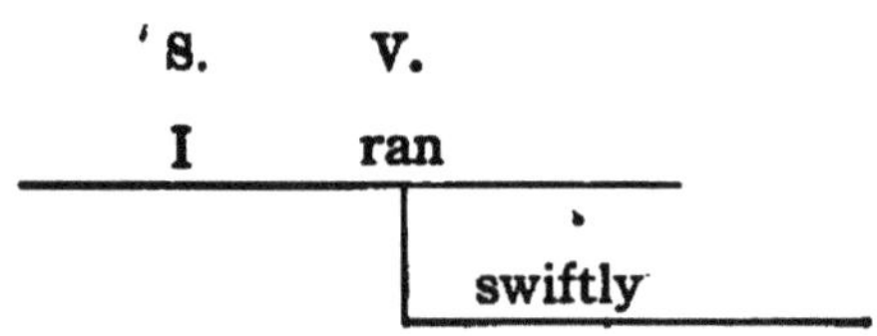

14. Adverbs: modifier of an adjective. [Buehler, §§ 43 ff., 85.]

You are *very* good.

SIMPLE SENTENCE

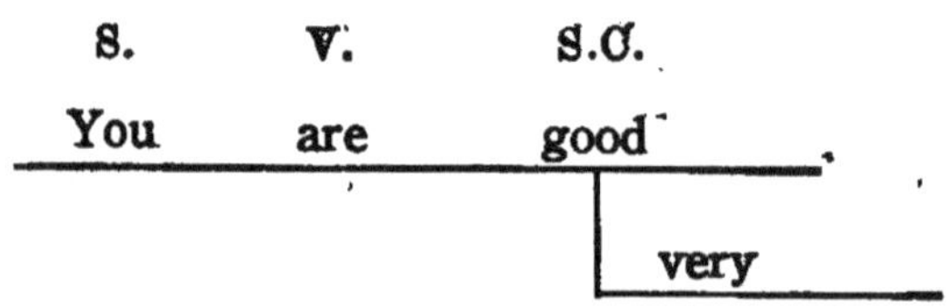

15. Adverbs: modifier of another adverb. [Buehler, §§ 43 ff., 85.]

I ran *very* swiftly.

SIMPLE SENTENCE

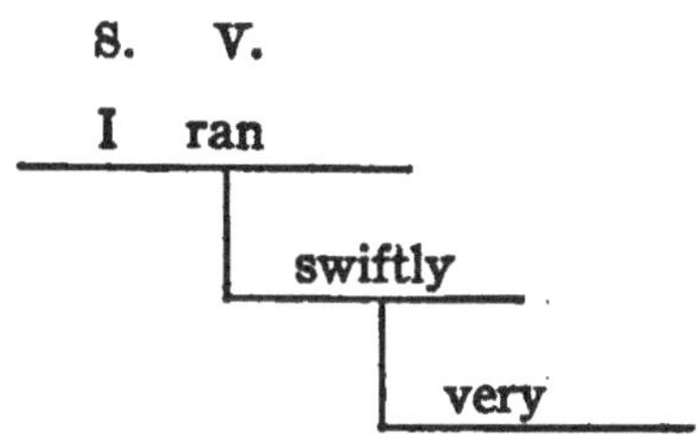

16. Prepositions: a preposition is sometimes an inseparable part of a passive verb, but should be taken separately whenever possible. [Buehler, § 239.]

Fulton was laughed *at*.
They laughed *at* Fulton.

SIMPLE SENTENCE

SIMPLE SENTENCE

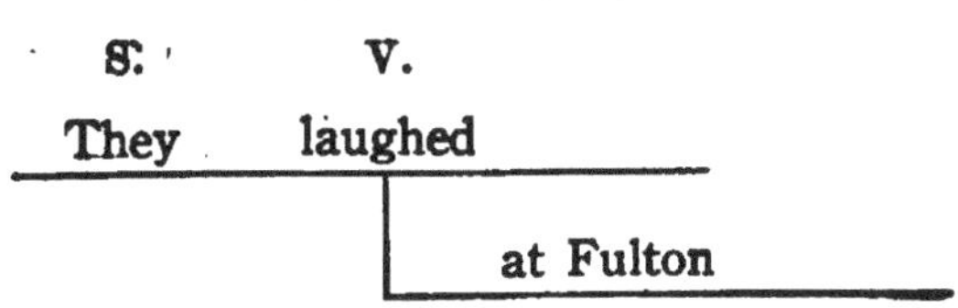

17. Prepositional Adverbs: a word, originally a preposition, may sometimes be used as an adverb. [Buehler, § 239.]

The arrow whistled *by*.

Simple Sentence

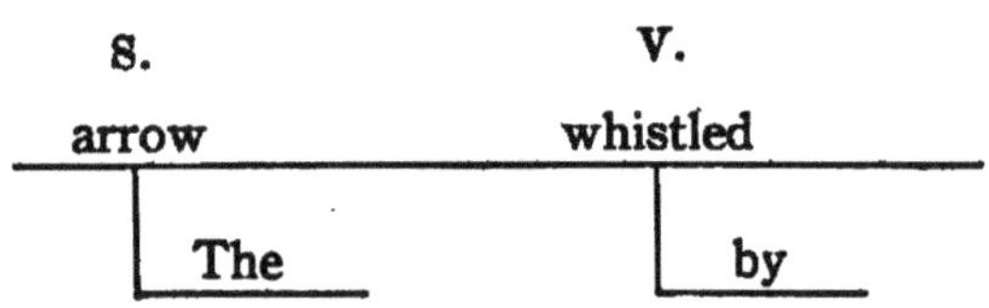

18. Relative Pronouns: subject in the relative clause. [Buehler, §§ 49, 144 ff.]

He is a man *who* is trustworthy.

Complex Sentence

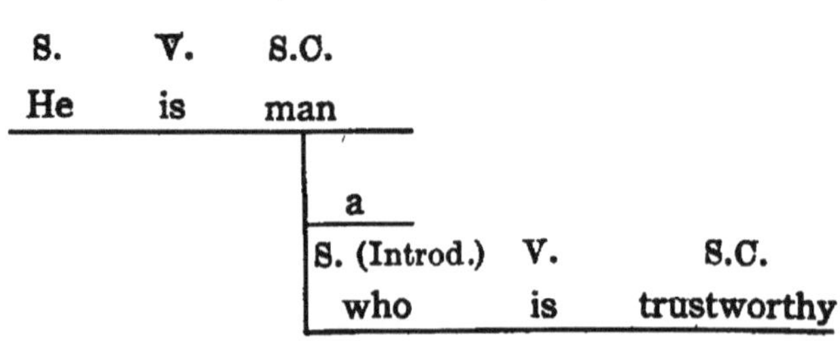

19. Relative Pronouns: object in the relative clause. [Buehler, §§ 49, 144 ff.]

He is a man *whom* I trust.

COMPLEX SENTENCE

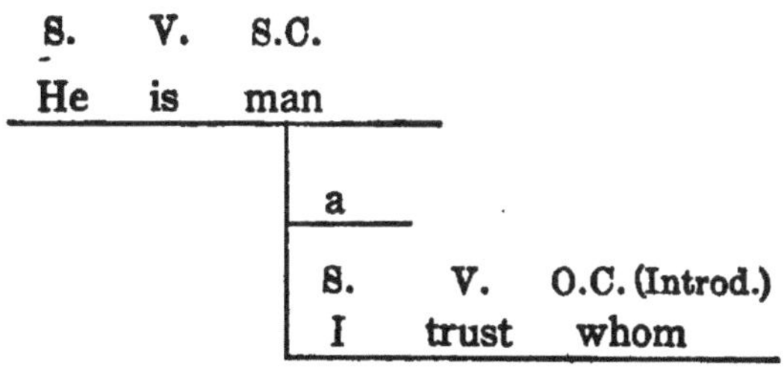

20. Relative Pronouns: retained object in the relative clause. [Buehler, §§ 49, 144 ff., 188.]

I have forgotten the message *which* I was given.

COMPLEX SENTENCE

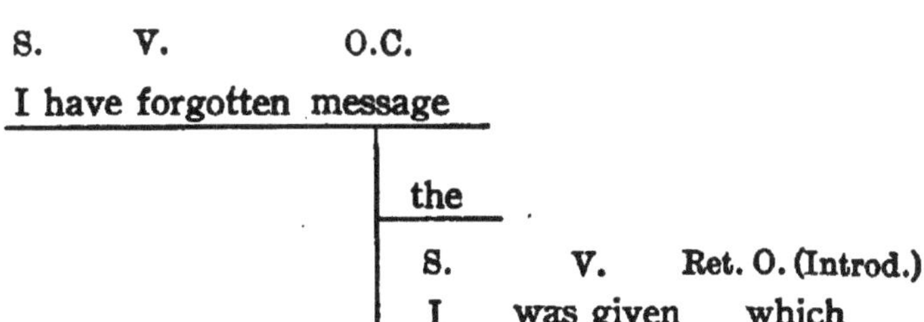

21. Relative Pronouns: subjective complement in the relative clause. [Buehler, §§ 49, 144 ff.]

His army was no longer the effective fighting force *that* it had been.

COMPLEX SENTENCE

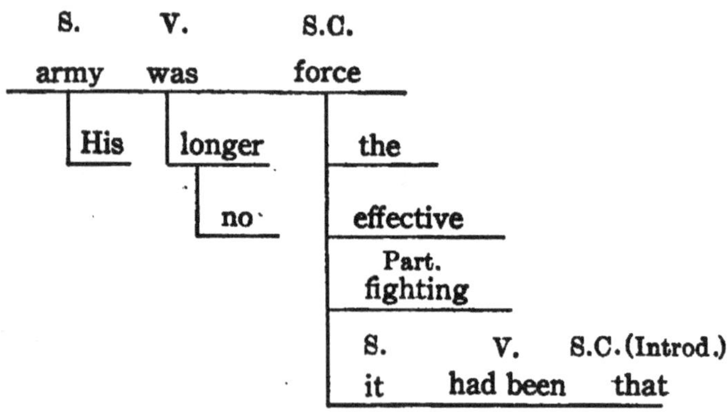

22. Relative Pronouns: objective complement in the relative clause. [Buehler, §§ 49, 144 ff.]

You will always be the same kind of person *that* you originally made yourself.

COMPLEX SENTENCE

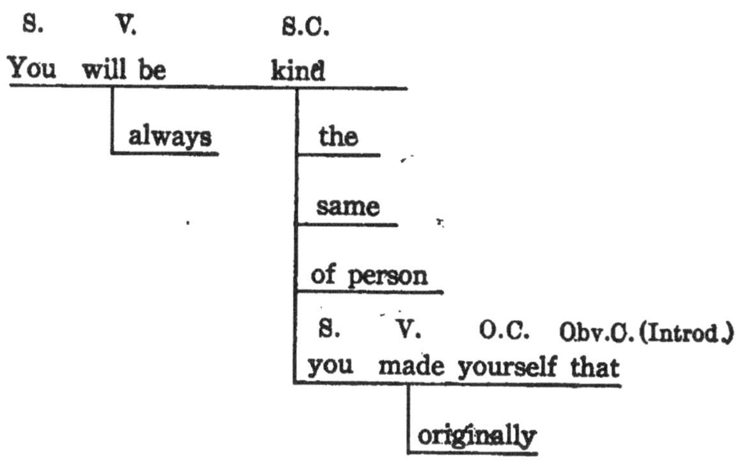

23. Relative Pronouns: secondary object in the relative clause. [Buehler, §§ 49, 53, 144 ff.]

These are the questions *which* you asked me.

COMPLEX SENTENCE

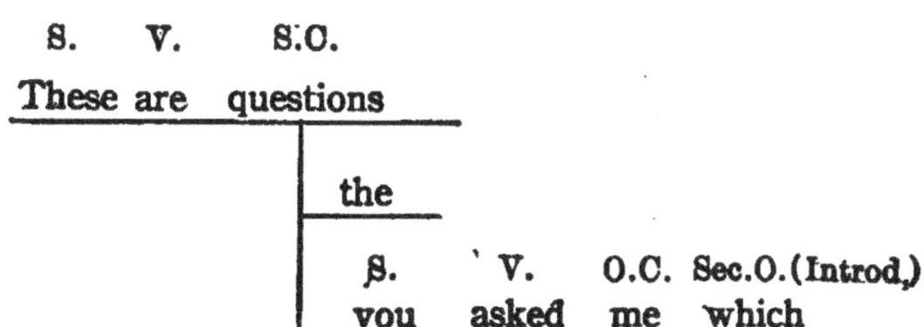

24. Relative Pronouns: possessive in the relative clause. [Buehler, §§ 49, 144 ff.]

He is a man *whose* name is famous.

COMPLEX SENTENCE

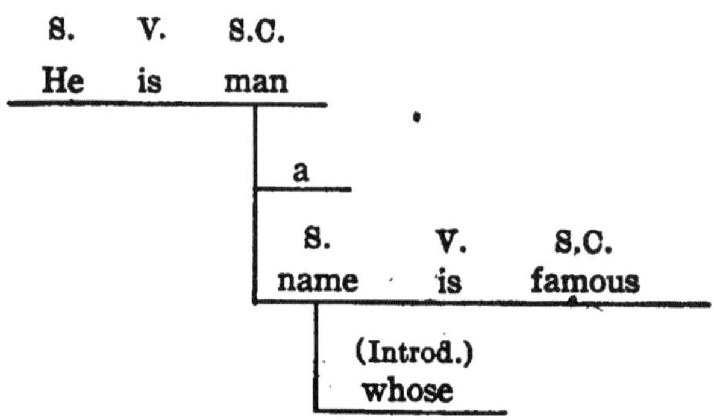

25. Relative Pronouns: object of a preposition in the relative clause. [Buehler, §§ 49, 144 ff.]

He is a man in *whom* I have confidence.

COMPLEX SENTENCE

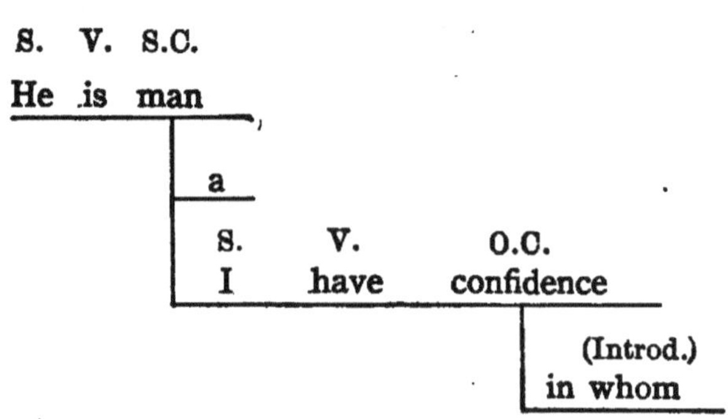

26. Relative Clauses containing their own antecedents, introduced by "whoever." [Buehler, §§ 49, 144 ff., 153.]

I shall question *whoever comes.*

COMPLEX SENTENCE

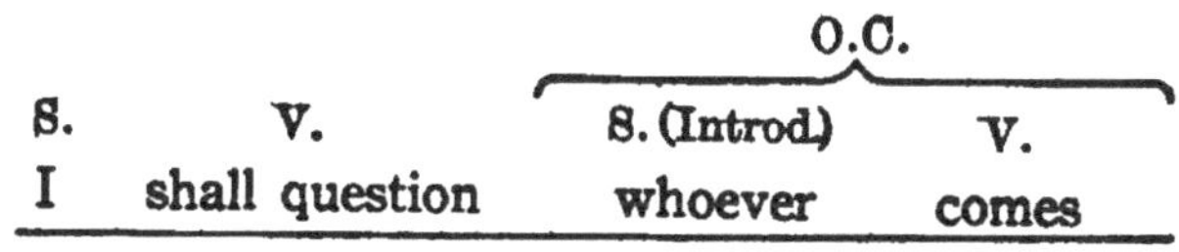

27. Relative Clauses containing their own antecedents, introduced by "what." [Buehler, §§ 49, 144 ff., 147.]

Often a man is unfairly judged by *what he says.*

COMPLEX SENTENCE

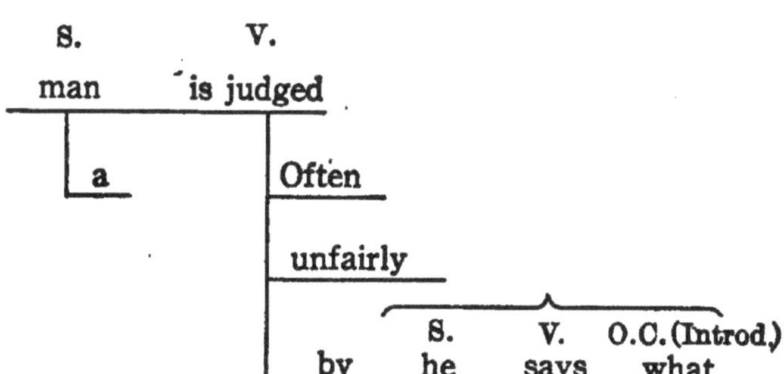

28. Conjunctions: coördinating conjunctions join expressions in the same construction. [Buehler, §§ 87, 242.]

Dishonest *or* ignorant citizens are dangerous to their neighbors, to the nation, *and* to the world.

Simple Sentence

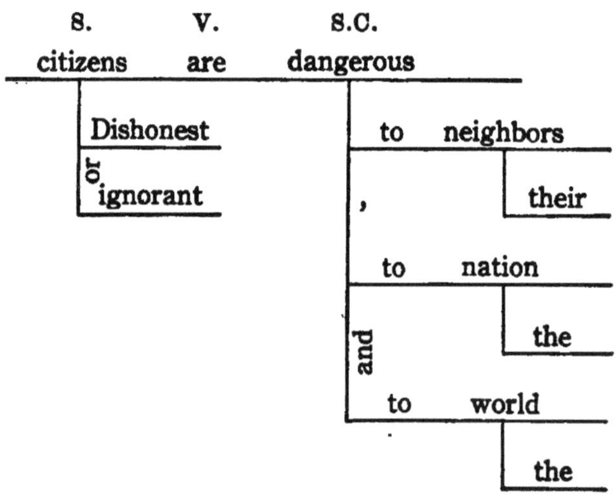

29. Preposition with Compound Object.

I walked in *fear* and *dread*.

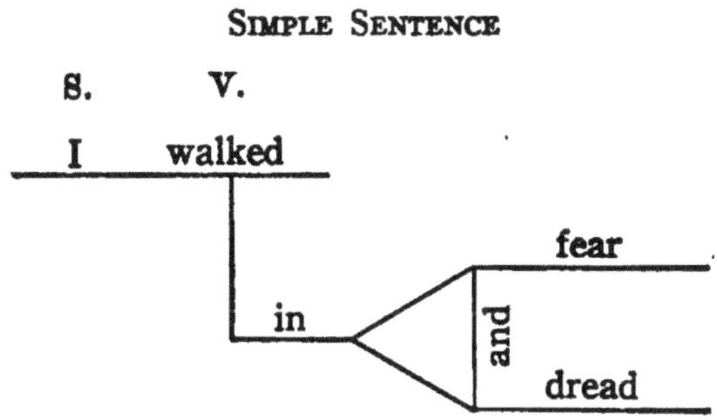

30. Simple Sentences: simple subject and simple predicate. [Buehler, § 70.]

I saw him twice.

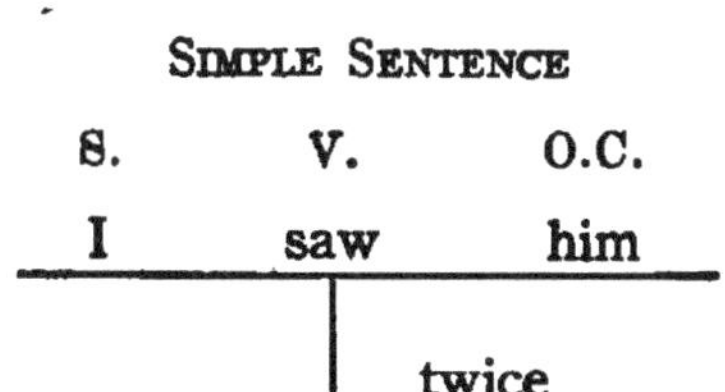

31. Simple Sentences: compound subject and simple predicate. [Buehler, § 70.]

You and I saw him twice.

SIMPLE SENTENCE

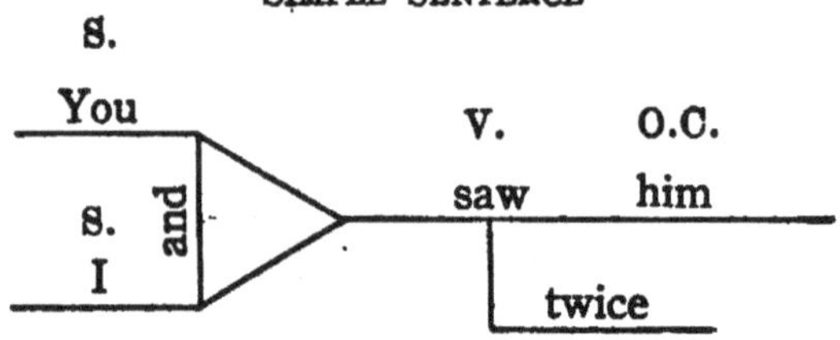

32. Simple Sentences: simple subject and compound predicate. [Buehler, § 70.]

I met him once, and saw him twice, but did not address him.

SIMPLE SENTENCE

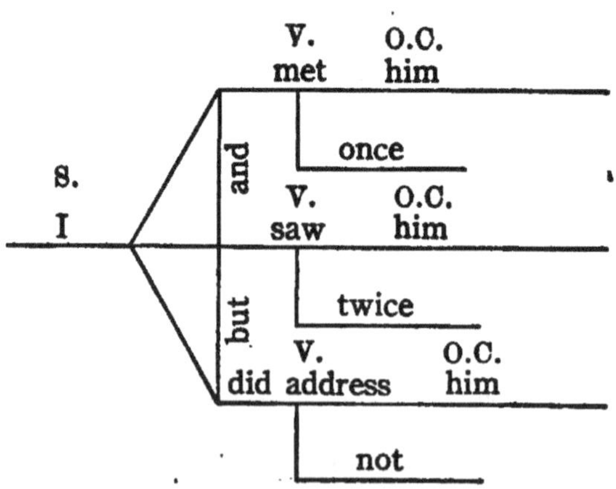

33. Simple Sentences: compound subject and compound predicate. [Buehler, § 70.]

Both you and I met him once, and saw him twice, but did not address him.

SIMPLE SENTENCE

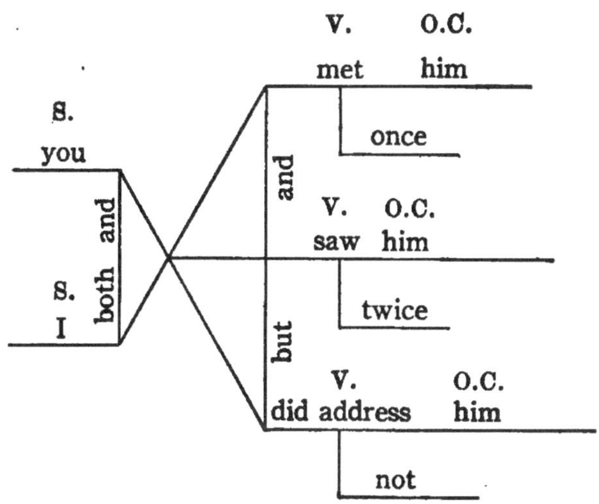

34. **Compound Sentences.** [Buehler, § 73.]

The rain descended, and the floods came.

COMPOUND SENTENCE

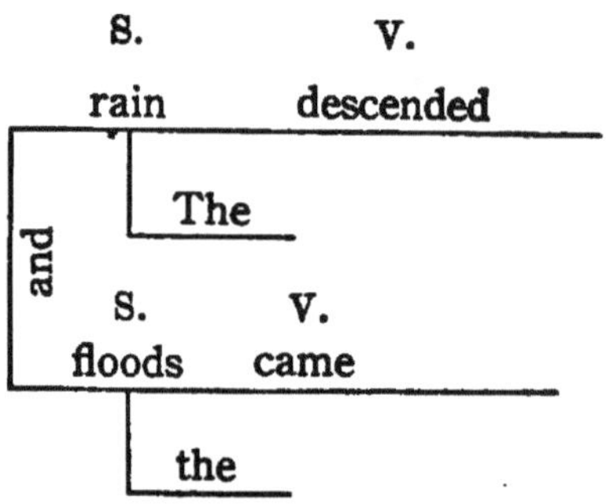

35. **Complex Sentences: subordinate clause used adjectivally.** [Buehler, §§ 49, 71.]

He is a man *whom I trust.*

COMPLEX SENTENCE

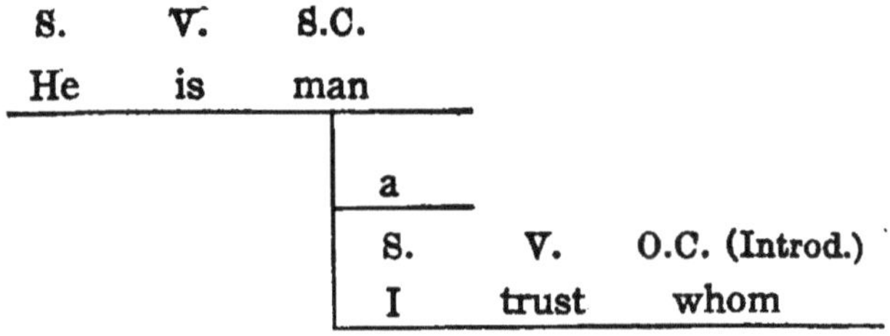

36. Complex Sentences: subordinate clauses, introduced by conjunctive adverbs ("where," "when," "while," etc.), used adjectivally. [Buehler, §§ 49, 71.]

The day *when he died* was stormy.

COMPLEX SENTENCE*

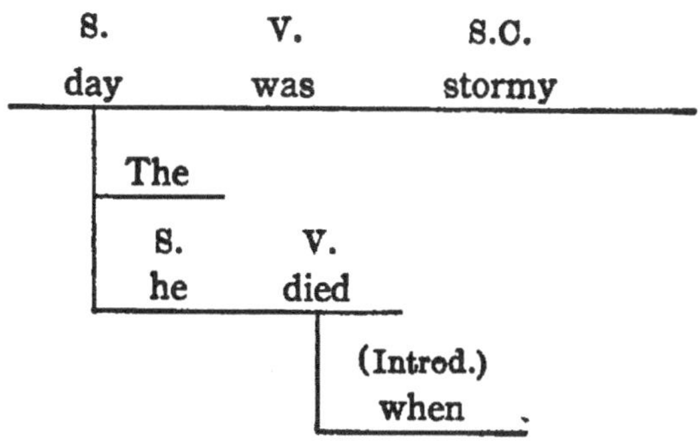

37. Complex Sentences: subordinate clauses used adverbially. [Buehler, §§ 49, 71.]

The windows, open *because the night was warm,* shone invitingly *when I entered the garden.*

COMPLEX SENTENCE

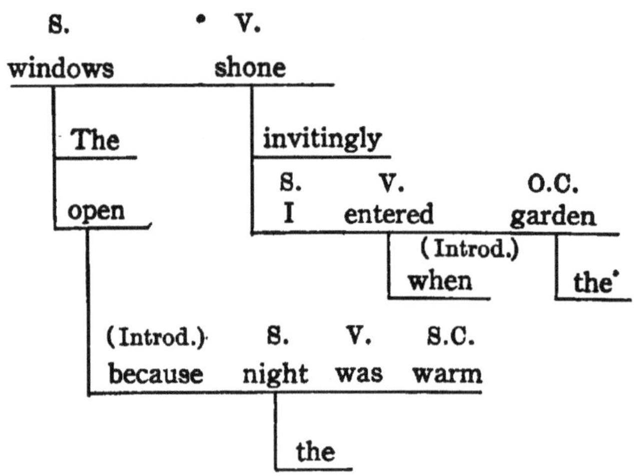

38. Complex Sentences: subordinate clause used substantively as subject. [Buehler, §§ 58, 71.]

That you have wronged me doth appear in this.

COMPLEX SENTENCE

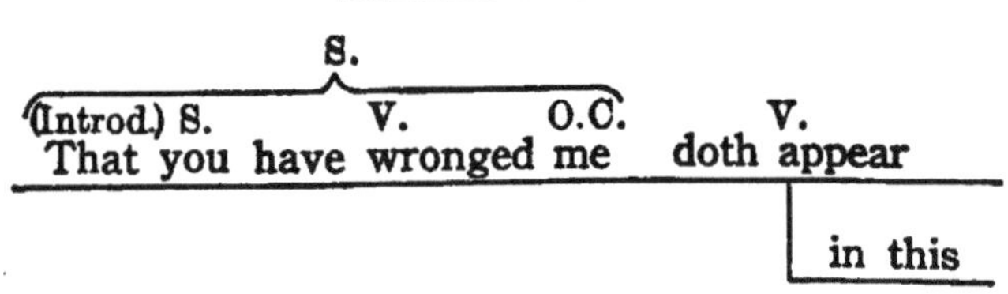

39. Complex Sentences: subordinate clause used substantively as complement. [Buehler, §§ 59, 71.]

Columbus did not know *that he had discovered a continent.*

COMPLEX SENTENCE

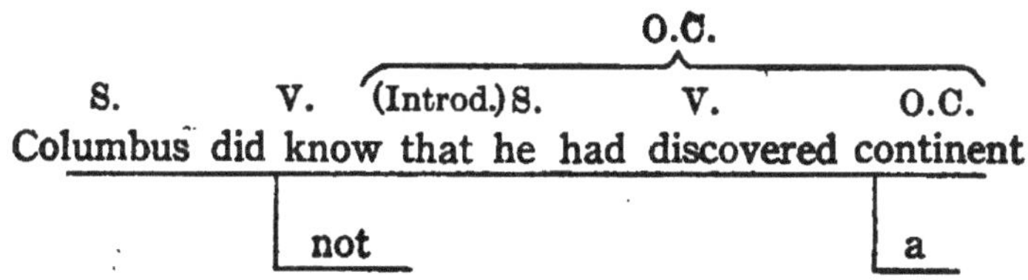

40. Complex Sentences: subordinate clause used substantively as appositive. [Buehler, §§ 60, 71.]

The fact *that lightning is identical with electricity* was demonstrated by Franklin.

COMPLEX SENTENCE

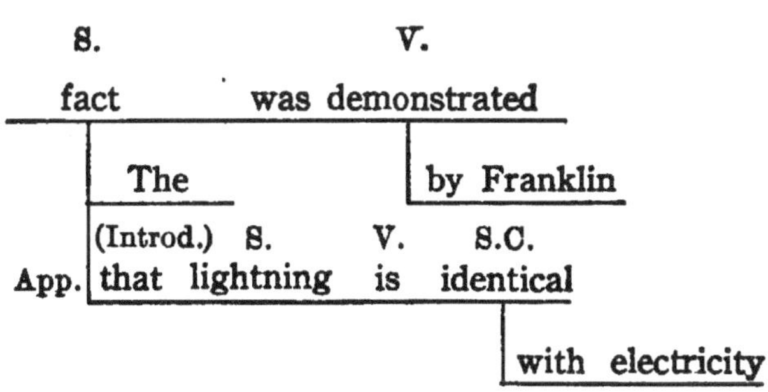

41. Compound-complex Sentences. [Buehler, § 73.]

Columbus did not know that he had discovered a continent, but Magellan proved it by his circumnavigation of the globe.

COMPOUND-COMPLEX SENTENCE

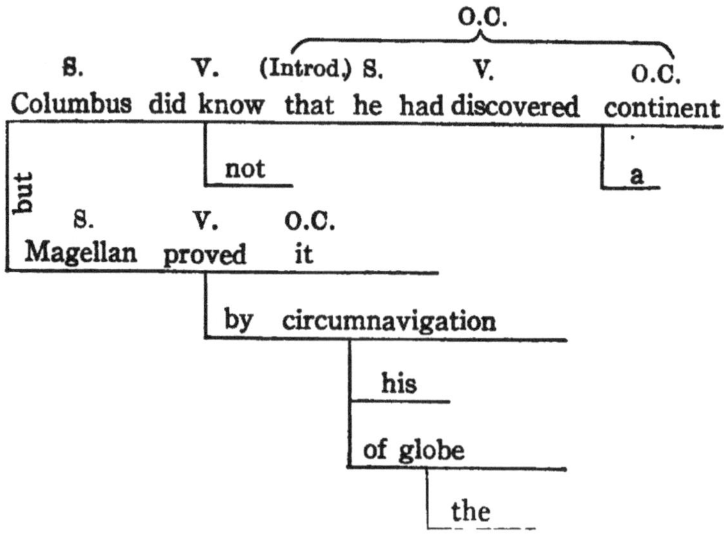

42. Direct Discourse, object of verb of saying. [Buehler, § 59.]

" He was a traitor," I answered, " and deserved no consideration."

Complex Sentence

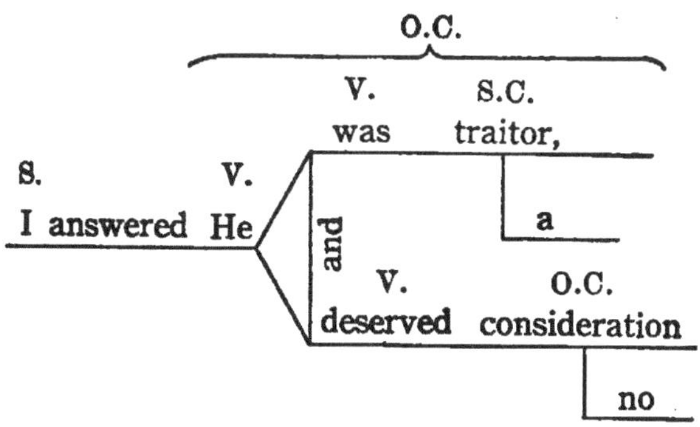

43. Coördinate Subordinate Clauses. [Buehler, §§ 171, 242.]

I smiled when he first opened his lips and while he told his story.

COMPLEX SENTENCE

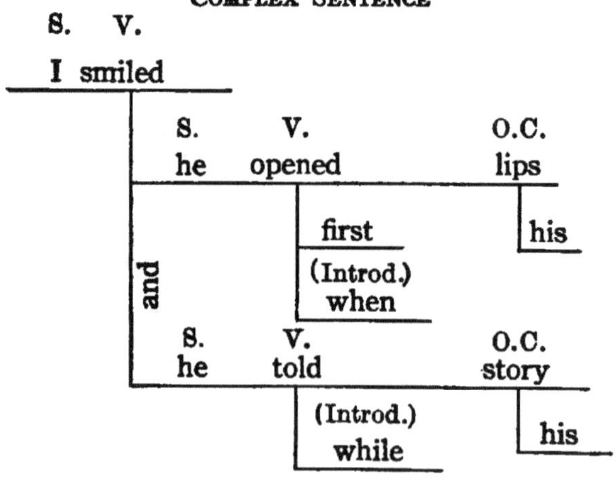

44. **Coördinate Subordinate Clauses, introduced by a single subordinating conjunction.** [Buehler, § 242.]

They listened to Franklin's advice because his words had always been moderate and his honesty had never been questioned.

COMPLEX SENTENCE

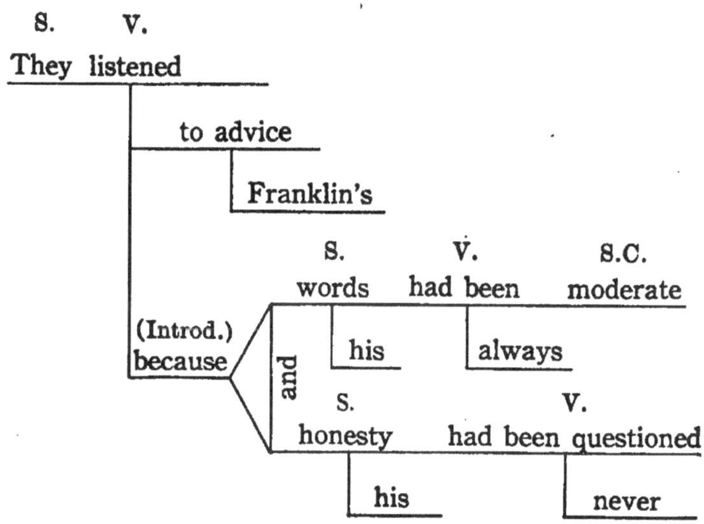

45. Diagramming, when more space is needed.

King Richard I. had hardly been expecting that a treacherous revolution was being rendered possible by his own brother.

COMPLEX SENTENCE

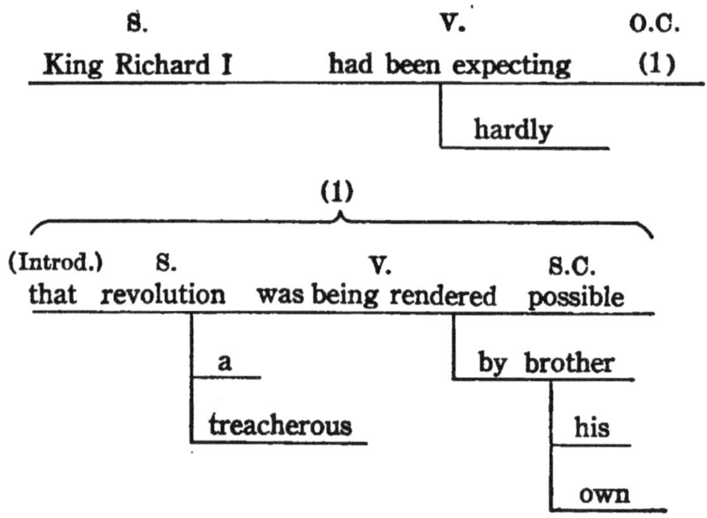

46. Direct Question, introduced by an interrogative pronoun or an interrogative adverb; to diagram, rearrange in the declarative order. [Buehler, §§ 143, 171.]

Who are you, and *when* can you come?

COMPOUND SENTENCE

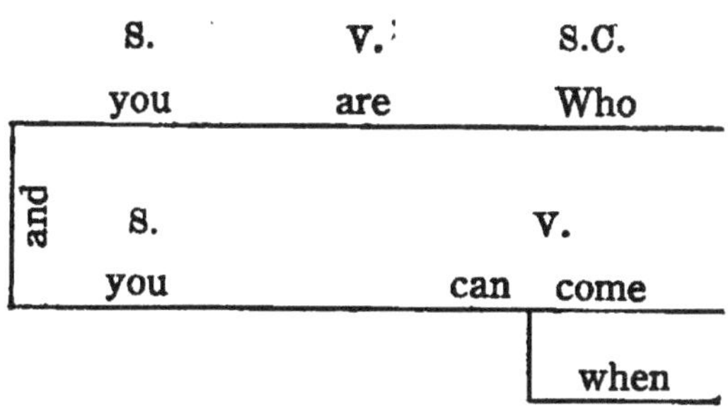

47. Indirect Question, introduced by an interrogative pronoun or an interrogative adverb, and forming a subordinate clause. [Buehler, §§ 143, 171.]

I will tell you *who* I am, but I don't know *when* I can come.

COMPOUND-COMPLEX SENTENCE

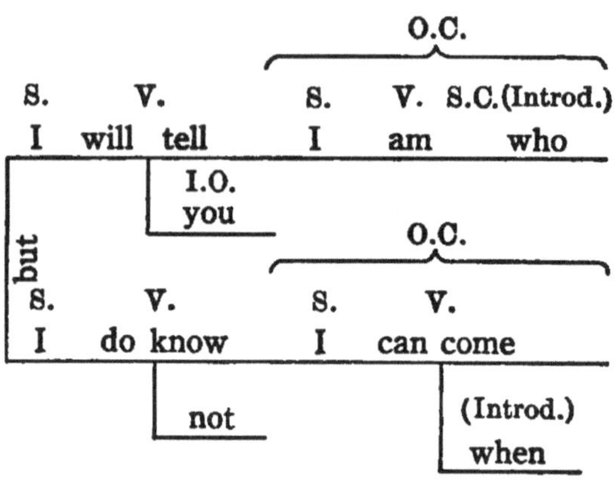

48. Correlatives, coördinating and phrasal. [Buehler, §§ 242, 243.]

They *not only* oppressed them, *but also* afterwards expelled them from Acadia.

Simple Sentence

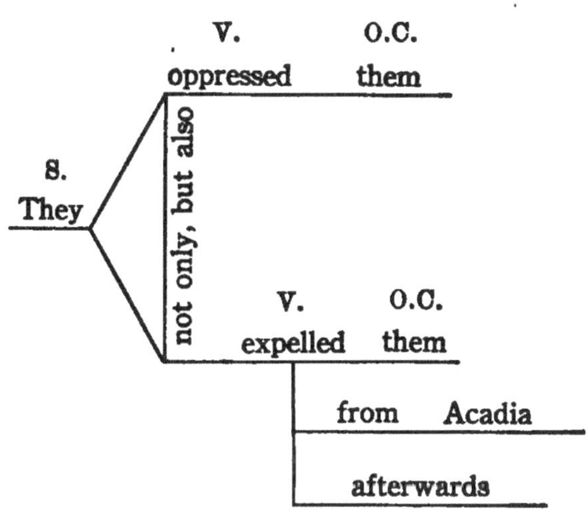

49. Correlatives: "as . . . as."

Jackson was *as* swift *as* McDowell was slow.

Complex Sentence

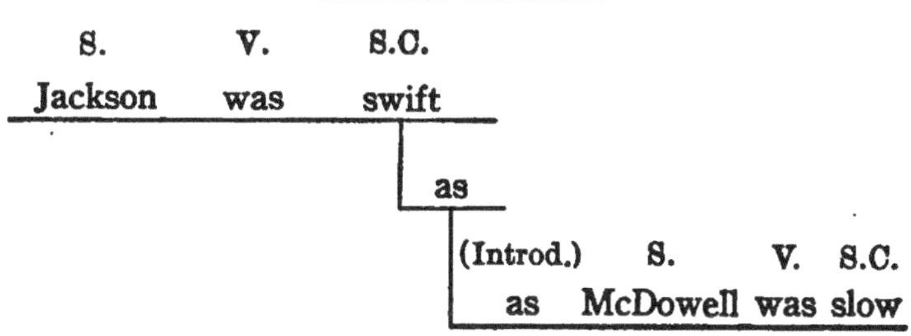

50. Ellipsis: subject of imperative verb. [Buehler, § 78.]

Do me a favor.

SIMPLE SENTENCE

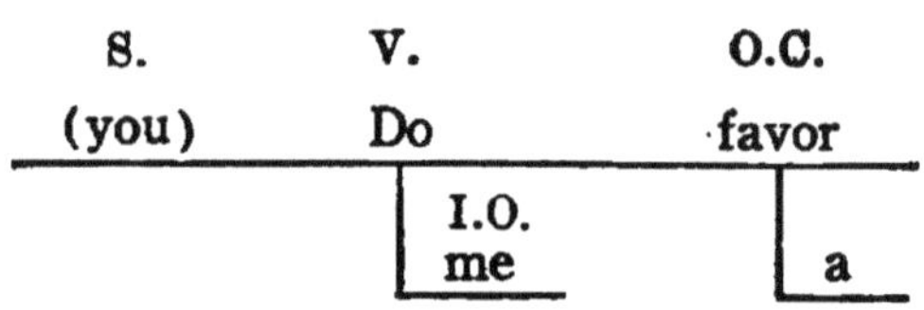

51. Ellipsis: after "than." [Buehler, § 78.]

He is taller than I.

COMPLEX SENTENCE

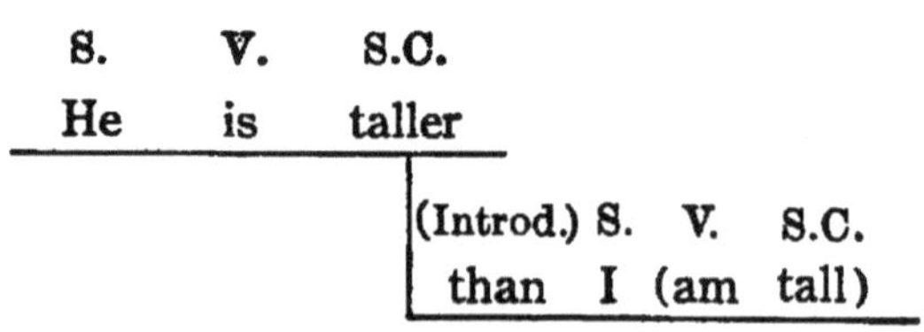

52. Ellipsis: after "as." [Buehler, § 78.]

He is as tall as I.

COMPLEX SENTENCE

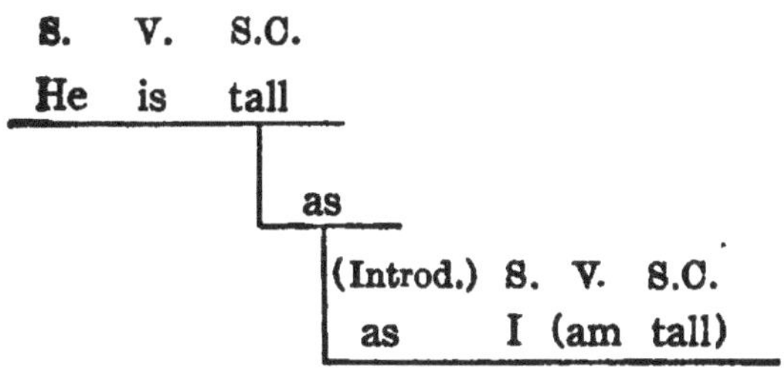

53. Ellipsis: after "as if." [Buehler, § 78.]

He acted as if mad.

COMPLEX SENTENCE

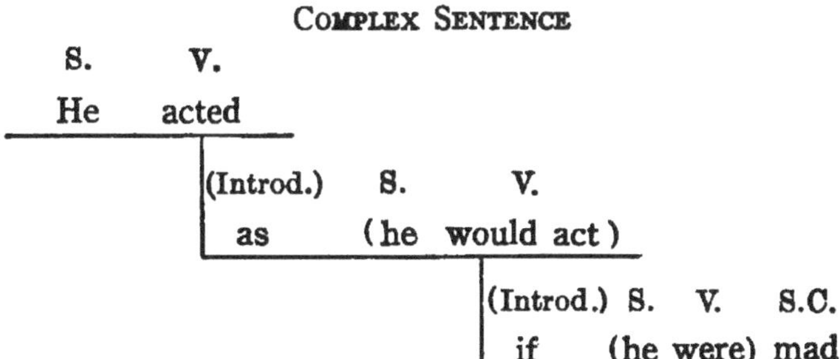

54. Ellipsis: relative pronoun. [Buehler, §§ 78, 151.]

This is the book I want.

COMPLEX SENTENCE

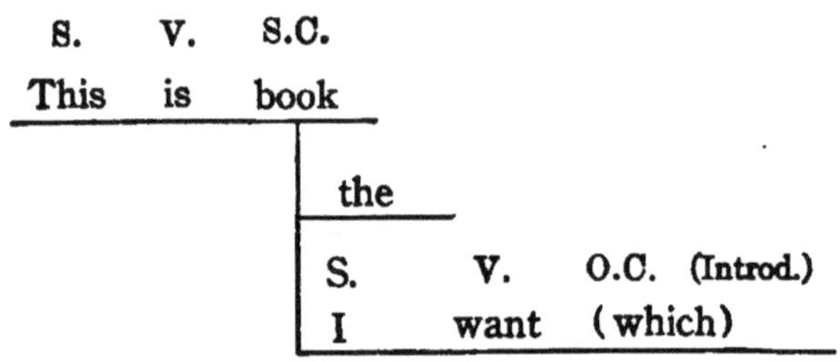

55. Ellipsis: when modifiers demand the presence of words which they may logically modify. [Buehler, § 78.]

He was a fool, *not* a wise man.

He ran to the station, and *buying* his ticket, boarded the train.

Simple Sentence

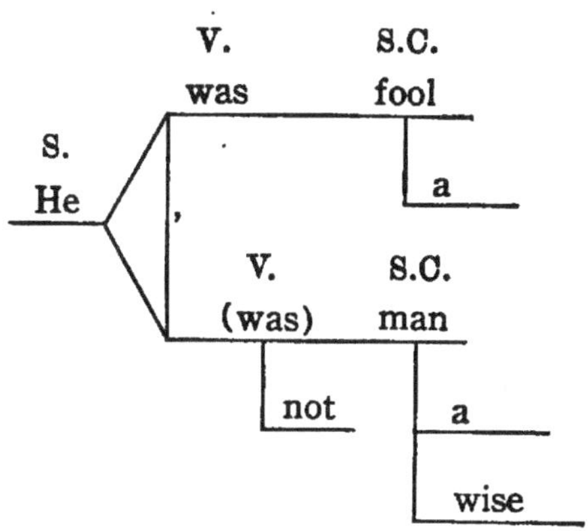

Compound Sentence

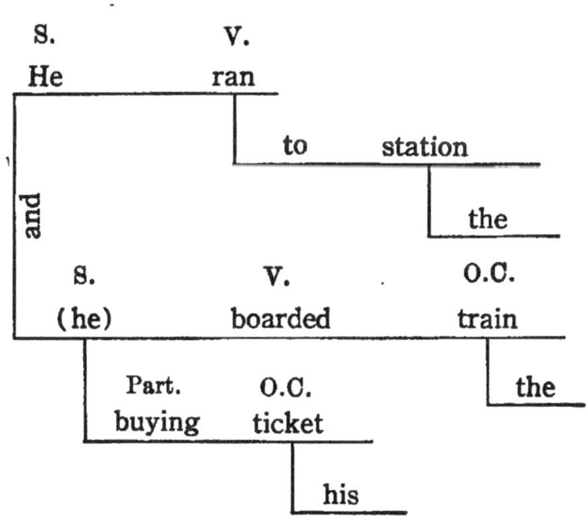

56. Infinitives: used substantively as subject. [Buehler, §§ 94, 229.]

To study [or, *Studying*] is hard.

[Note that in this sentence, and in sentences 57, 58, 60, and 61, either form of the infinitive could be used — with *to* or in *-ing*, as *to study* or *studying*.]

SIMPLE SENTENCE

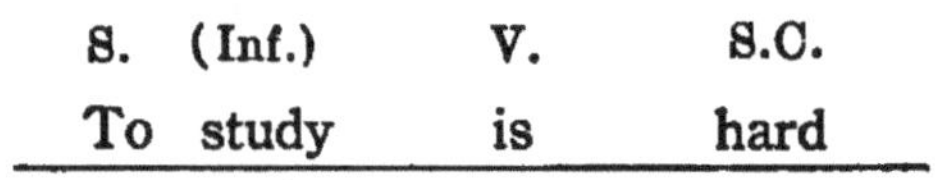

57. Infinitives: used substantively as object complement. [Buehler, §§ 94, 229.]

I hate *to study*.

SIMPLE SENTENCE

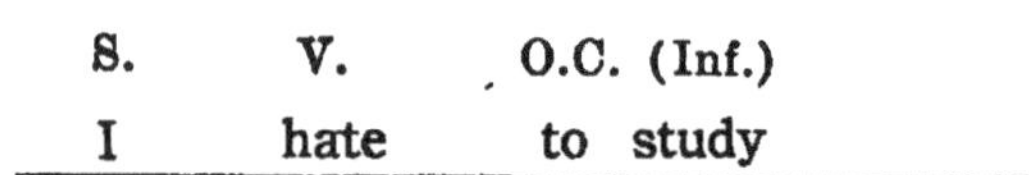

58. Infinitives: used substantively as subjective complement. [Buehler, §§ 94, 229.]

My duty is *to study*.

SIMPLE SENTENCE

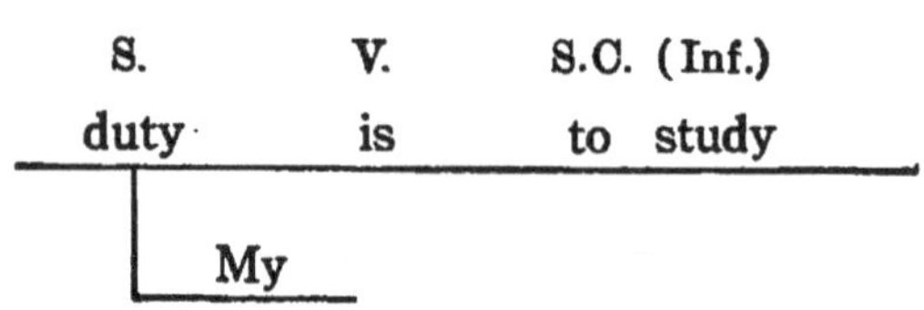

59. Infinitives: used substantively as secondary object. [Buehler, §§ 94, 229.]

I asked him *to read*.

SIMPLE SENTENCE

S.	V.	O.C.	Sec. O. (Inf.)
I	asked	him	to read

60. Infinitives: used substantively as appositive. [Buehler, §§ 94, 229.]

My duty, *to study*, is hard.

SIMPLE SENTENCE

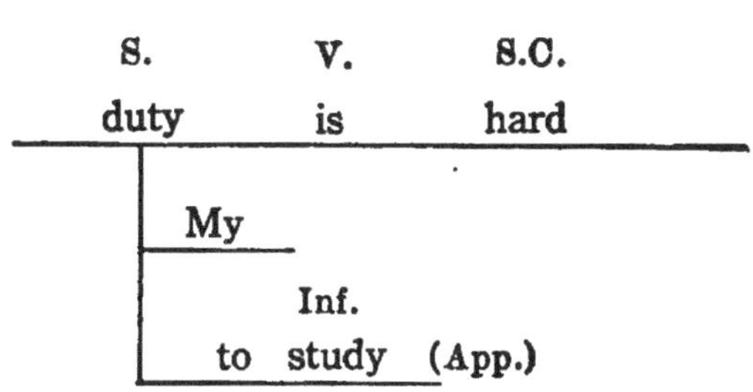

61. Infinitives: used substantively as object of a preposition. [Buehler, §§ 94, 229.]

He had no choice except *to obey*.

SIMPLE SENTENCE

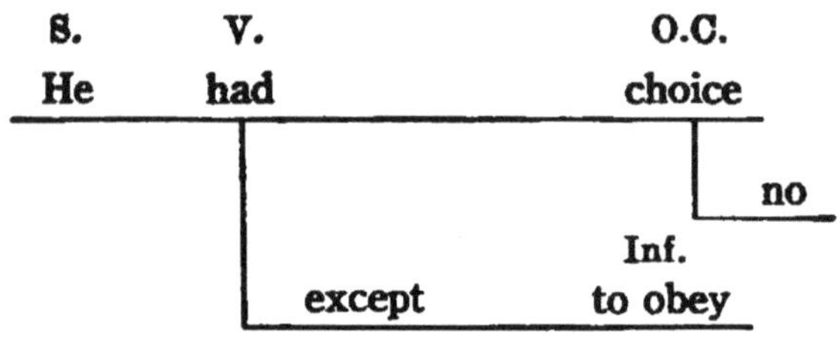

62. Infinitives: used adverbially to express purpose. [Buehler, §§ 94, 229.]

I came here *to study*.

SIMPLE SENTENCE

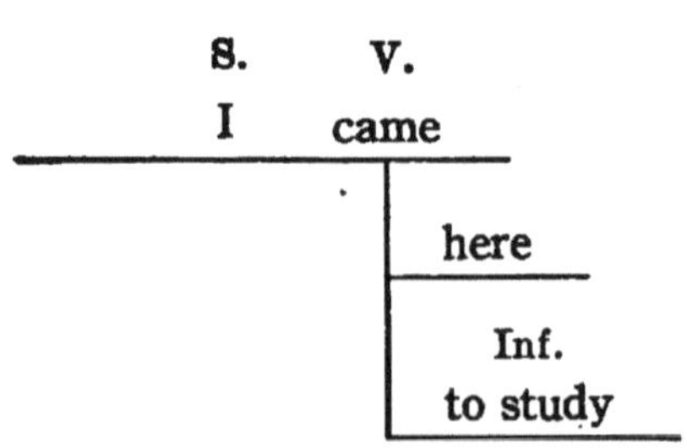

63. Infinitives: used adverbially to express specification. [Buehler, §§ 94, 229.]

My lesson is hard *to study*.

SIMPLE SENTENCE

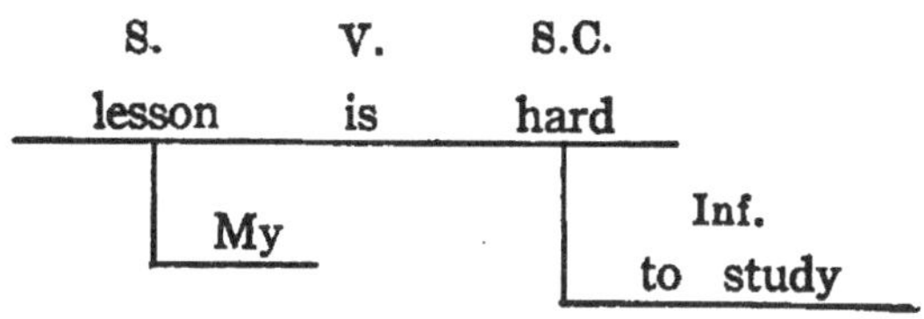

64. Infinitives: used adjectivally. [Buehler, §§ 94, 229.]

Now is the time *to study*.

SIMPLE SENTENCE

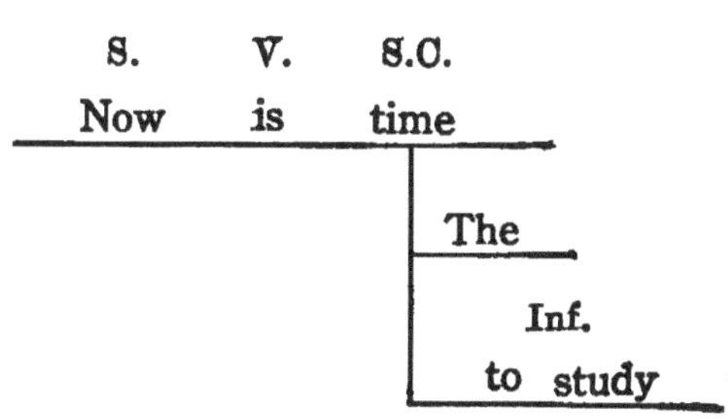

65. Participles: used adjectivally as modifier of a noun or pronoun. [Buehler, §§ 93, 222.]

A *rolling* stone gathers no moss.

SIMPLE SENTENCE

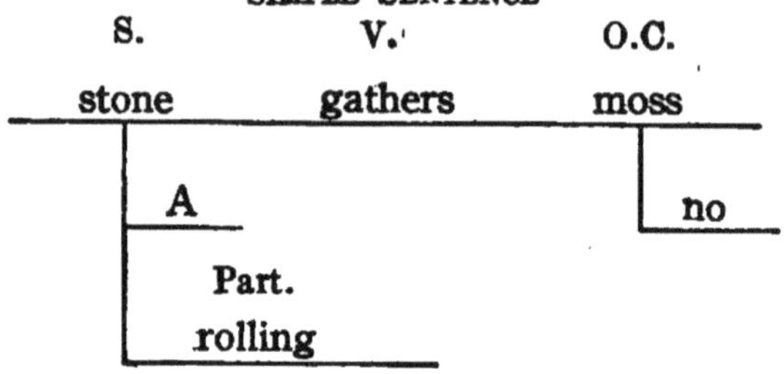

66. Participles: used adjectivally as subjective complement. [Buehler, §§ 93, 222.]

The soldiers are *tired.*

SIMPLE SENTENCE

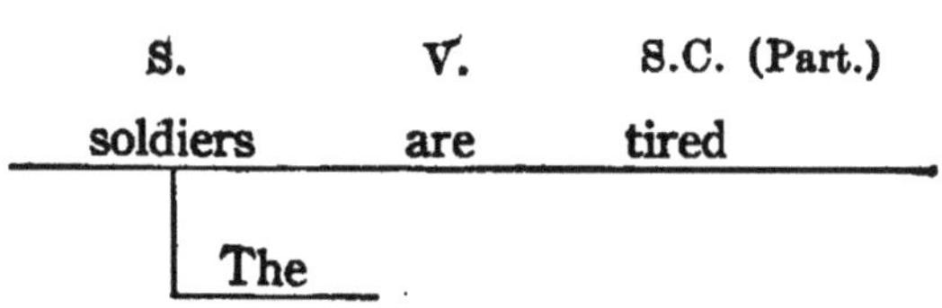

67. Participles: used adjectivally as subjective complement; note that if the participle stood before the subject, its construction and meaning would be simply those of a modifier. [Buehler, §§ 93, 222.]

The coffee was served *smoking*.
A boy came *sauntering* down the street.

SIMPLE SENTENCE

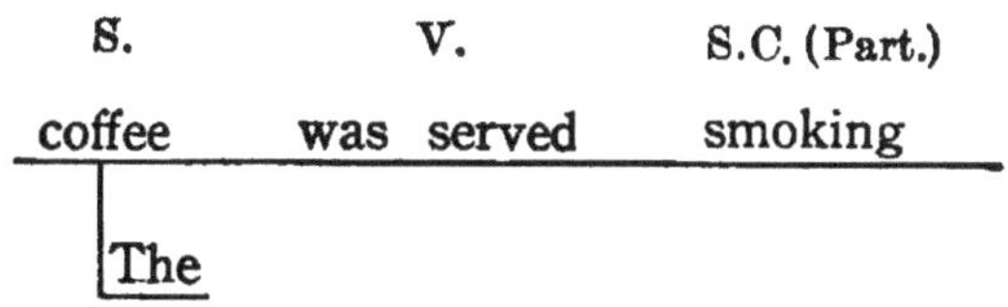

SIMPLE SENTENCE

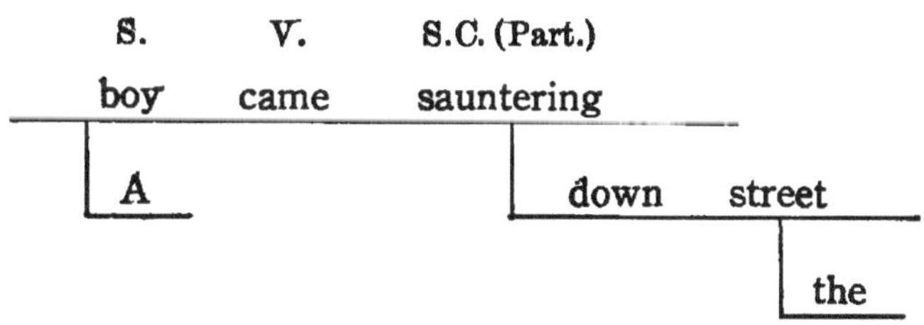

68. Participles: used adjectivally as objective complement. [Buehler, §§ 93, 222.]

I could scarcely make myself *heard.*

SIMPLE SENTENCE

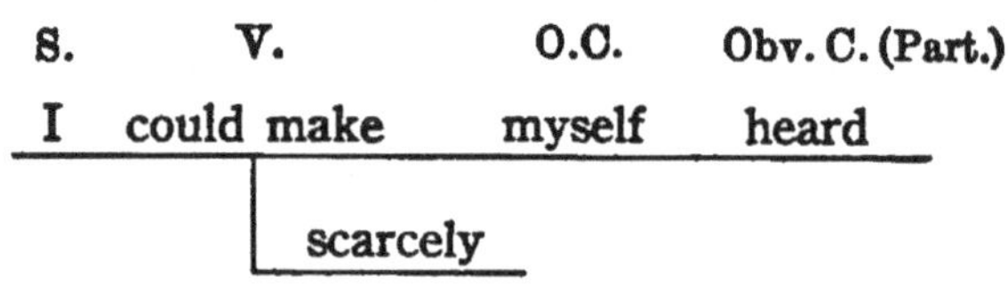

69. Infinitives: used as predicate of an infinitive clause. (Compare with sentence 70.) [Buehler, § 230.]

I saw a man *enter.*

COMPLEX SENTENCE

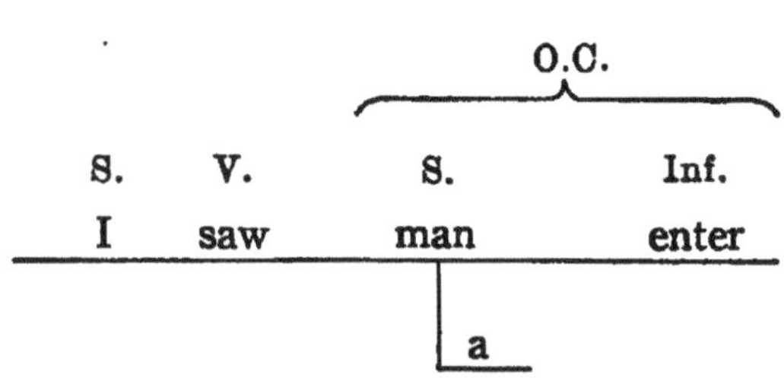

70. Participles: used as modifier of an object. (Compare with sentence 69.) [Buehler, §§ 93, 222.]

I saw a man *entering*.

SIMPLE SENTENCE

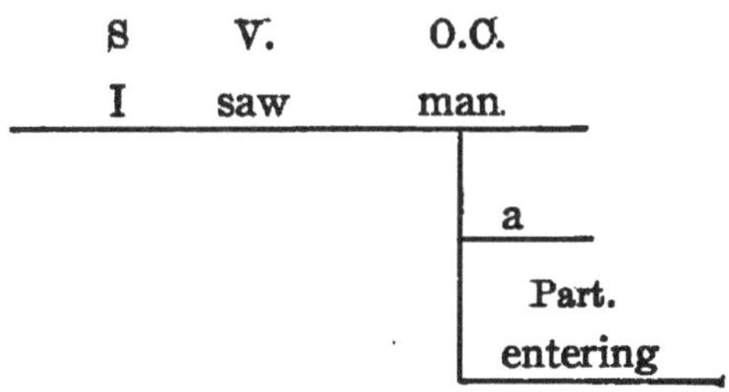

71. Object Complement of a Vèrbal. [Buehler, §§ 93, 94.]

I hate to study my *lessons*.

SIMPLE SENTENCE

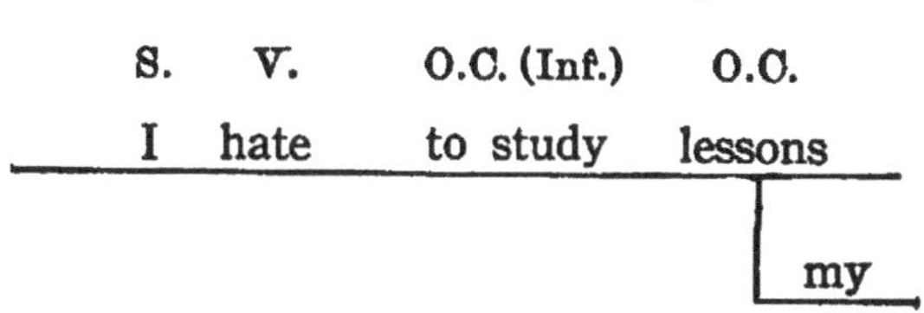

72. Subjective Complement of a Verbal. [Buehler, §§ 93, 94.]

John, feeling *ill*, retired.

SIMPLE SENTENCE

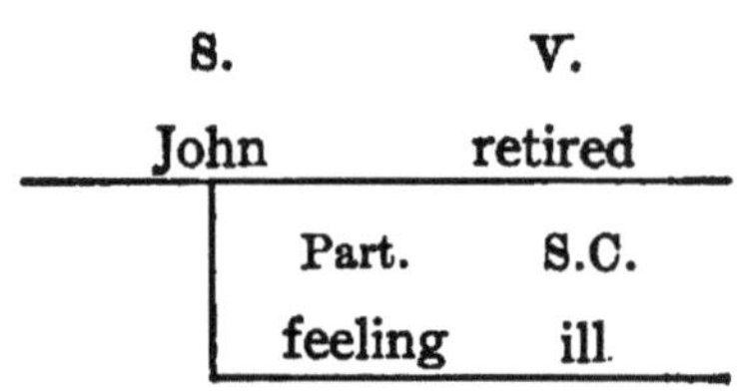

73. Objective Complement of a Verbal. [Buehler, §§ 93, 94.]

One exercises to make himself *strong*.

SIMPLE SENTENCE

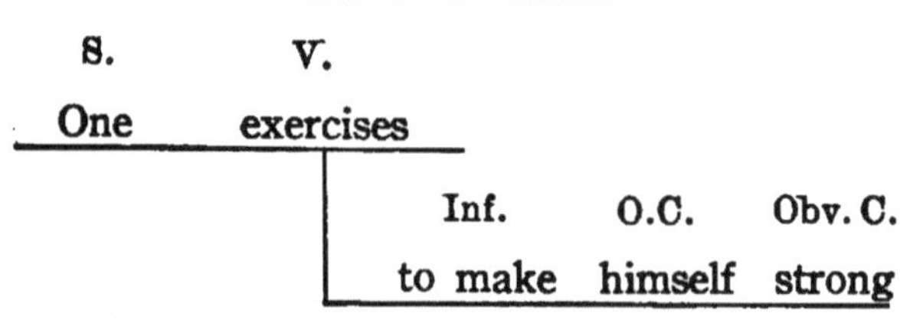

74. When a modifier might logically modify any one of a number of different expressions, choose the nearest. [Buehler, § 43 ff.]

Lose thyself in the continuous woods *where rolls the Oregon.*

COMPLEX SENTENCE

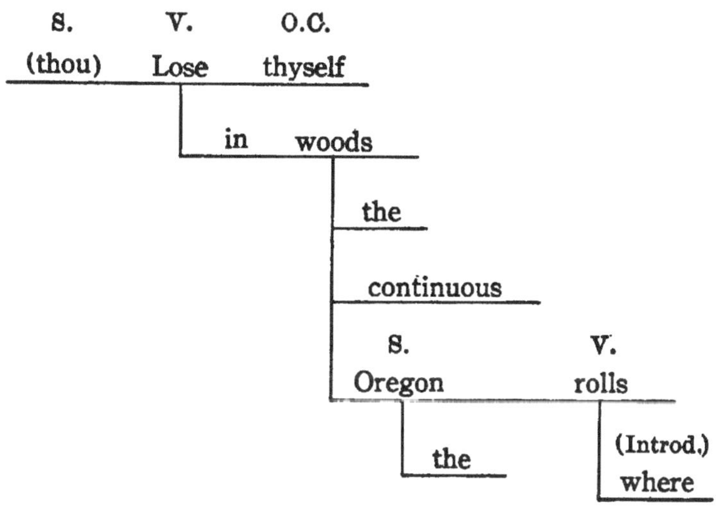

75. A single modifier that modifies two or more different expressions. [Buehler, § 43 ff.]

He worked and played, loved and fought, *with the same enthusiasm.*

SIMPLE SENTENCE

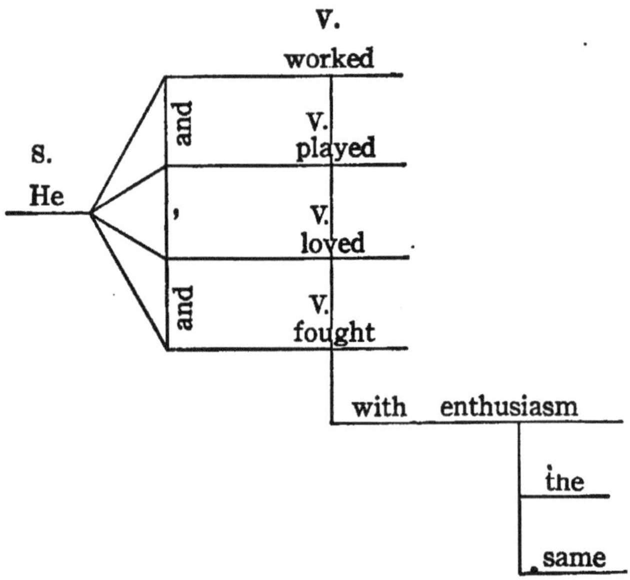

76. Hyphenated expressions are to be regarded as solid.

We need more *men-of-war.*

Simple Sentence

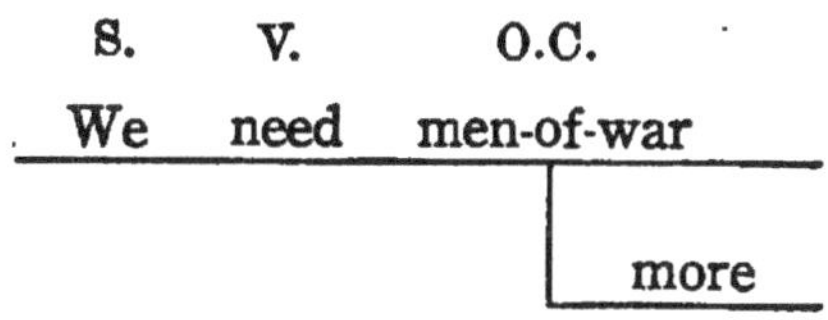

77. Titles, no matter how lengthy, are to be regarded as part of the names to which they are prefixed.

Vice-President John Tyler succeeded to the presidency.

Simple Sentence

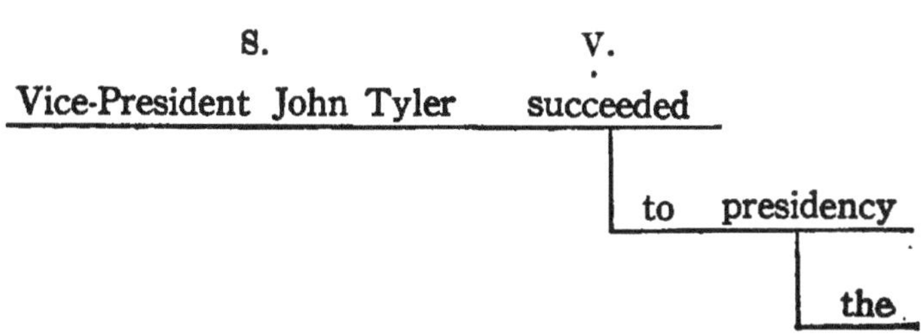

78. Nouns: used adjectivally; in this construction the noun has no case.

I saw a flock of *mountain* sheep.

Simple Sentence

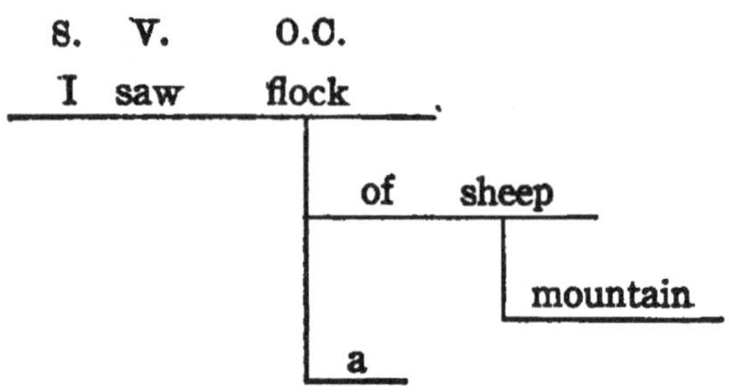

79. Nouns: used adverbially to express measure. [Buehler, §§ 115, 178.]

He travelled through Europe three *times*, walking *thousands* of miles, and staying *months* at a single place; yet his trips never cost a *penny*.

COMPOUND SENTENCE

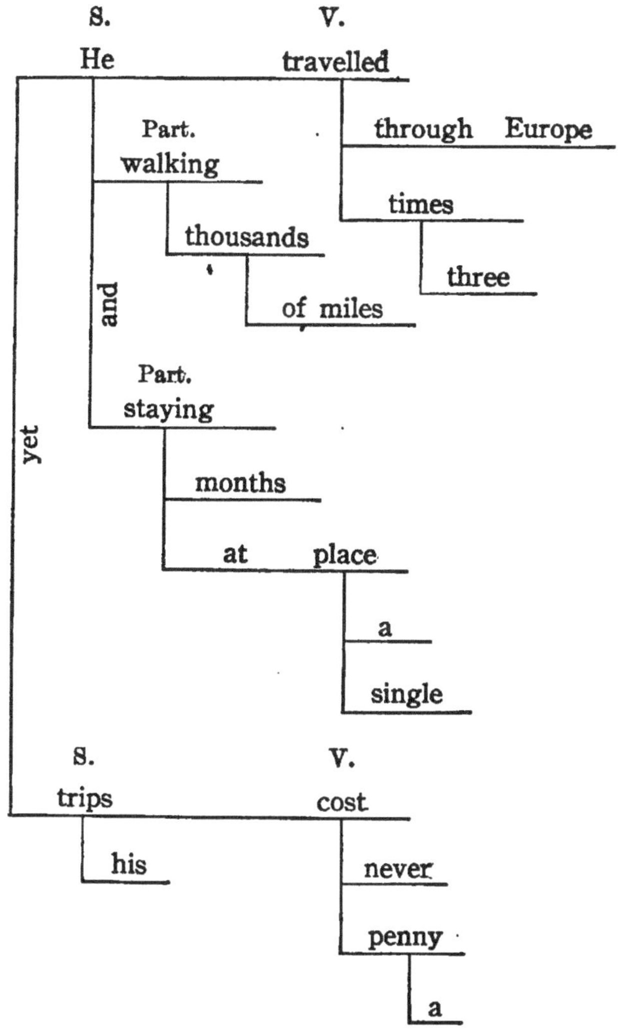

80. Independent Elements: vocative. [Buehler, §§ 62, 114.]

You, my dear *sir*, are my friend.

SIMPLE SENTENCE

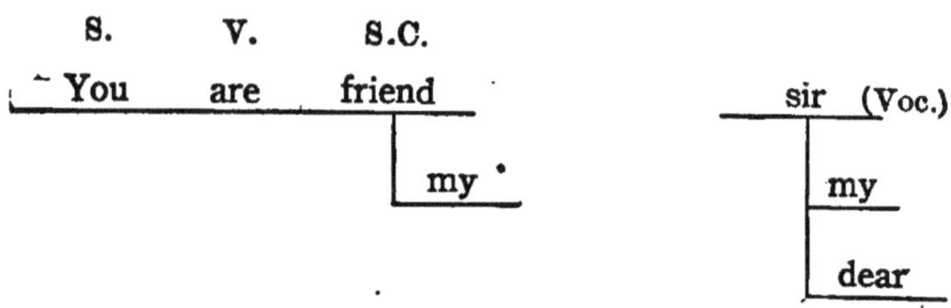

81. Independent Elements: exclamation. [Buehler, § 64.]

Oh, how it hurts!

SIMPLE SENTENCE

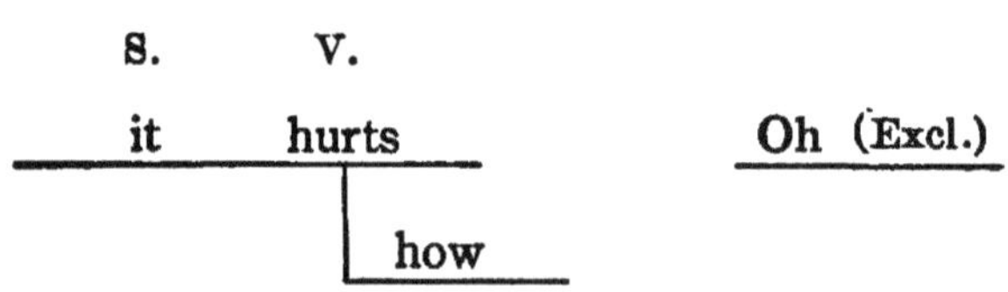

82. Independent Elements: pleonasm. [Buehler, § 68.]

The *smith*, a mighty man is he.

SIMPLE SENTENCE

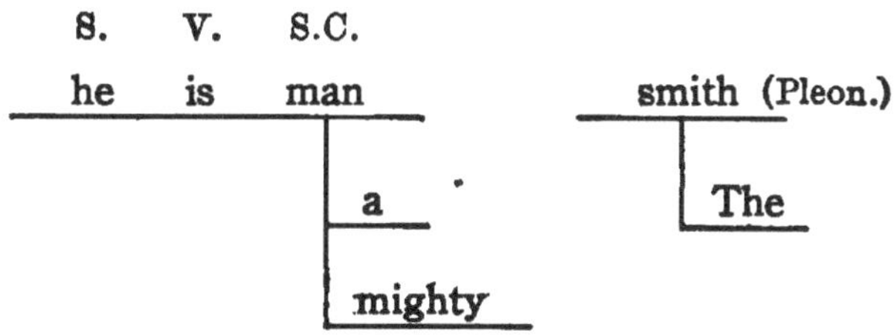

83. Independent Elements: parenthetical expression. [Buehler, § 66.]

This, *to be sure*, is no answer.

SIMPLE SENTENCE

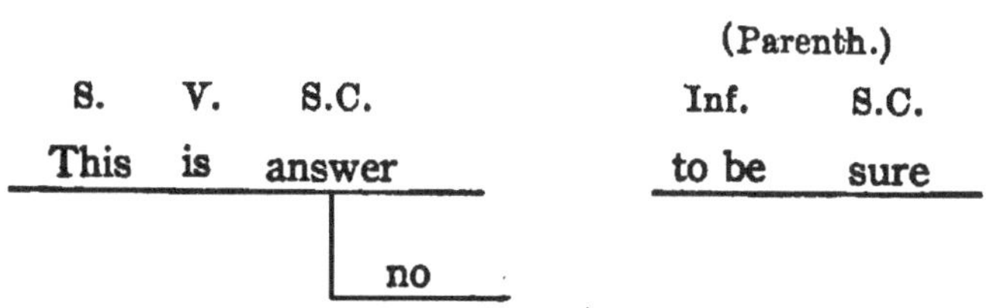

84. Independent Elements: nominative absolute. [Buehler, §§ 114, 223.]

His task performed, he did not rest content.

SIMPLE SENTENCE

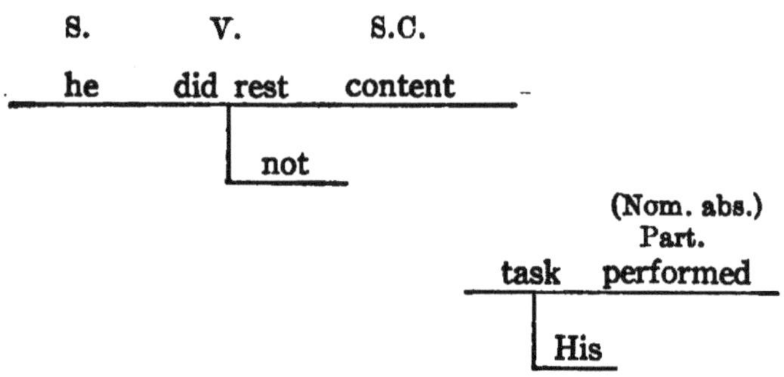

85. Independent Elements: nominative absolute in elliptical form. [Buehler, §§ 78, 114, 223.]

All Asia his, Alexander sighed for more worlds to conquer.

SIMPLE SENTENCE

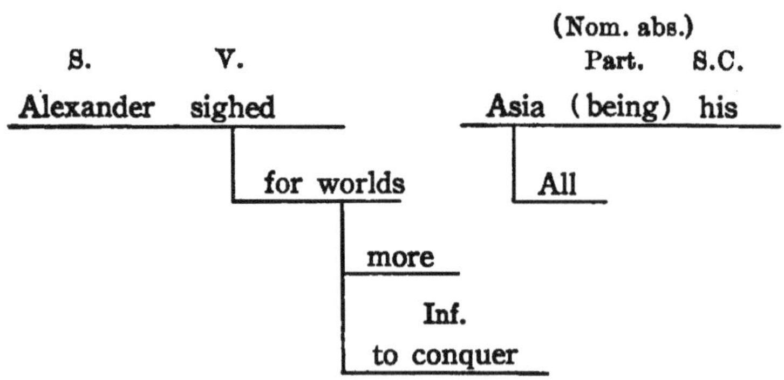

86. Substantive Adjectives. [Buehler, § 120.]

None but the *brave* deserves the *fair.*

SIMPLE SENTENCE

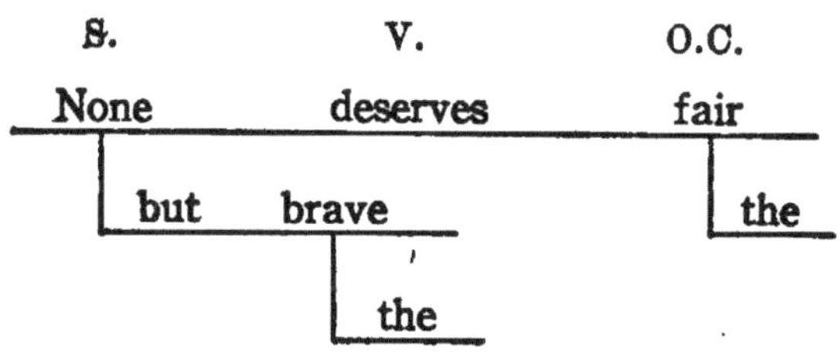

87. Adverbs: modifier of a phrase. [Buehler, § 43 ff.]

Is he a man *deeply* in your debt?

SIMPLE SENTENCE

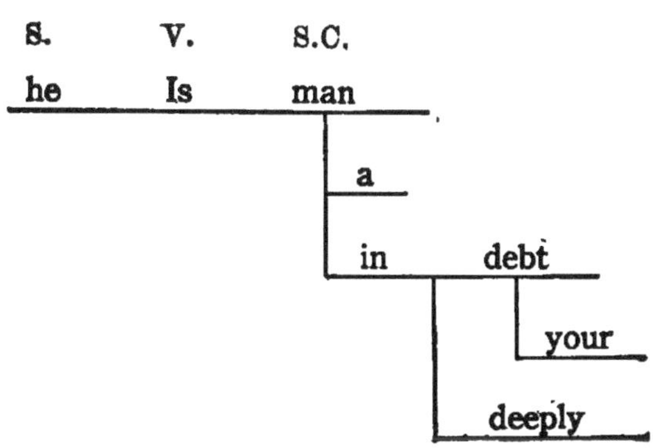

88. Adverbs: modifier of a clause. [Buehler, § 43 ff.]

Precisely when the clock struck twelve, the ghost appeared.

COMPLEX SENTENCE

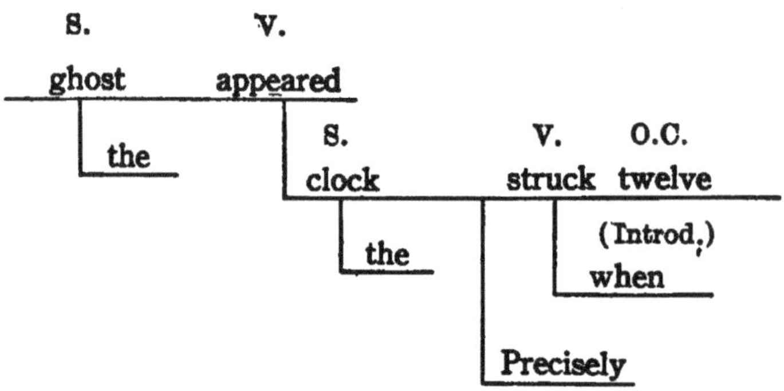

89. "As" used as a Relative Pronoun. [Buehler, § 150.]

I have the same trouble *as* you have.

COMPLEX SENTENCE

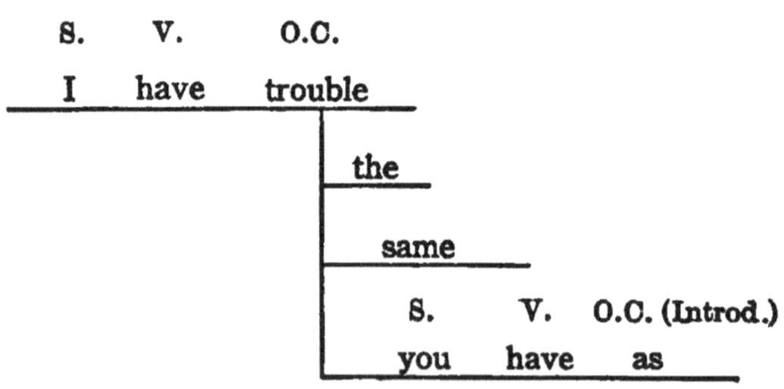

90. "But" used as a Relative Pronoun. [Buehler, § 150.]

Never was a villain known *but* had some goodness in him.

Complex Sentence

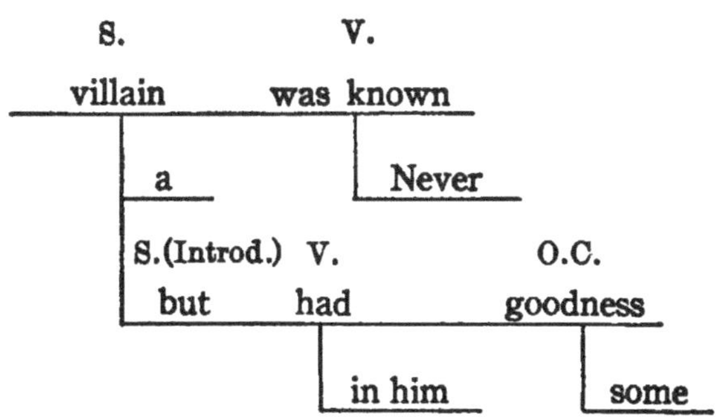

91. "It" Expletive. [Buehler, § 131.]

It is good that you are here.

Complex Sentence

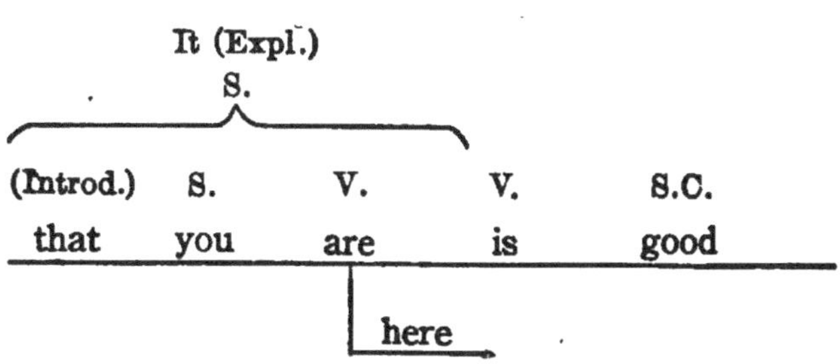

92. "There" Expletive. [Buehler, § 176.]

There was once a Greek Empire.

SIMPLE SENTENCE

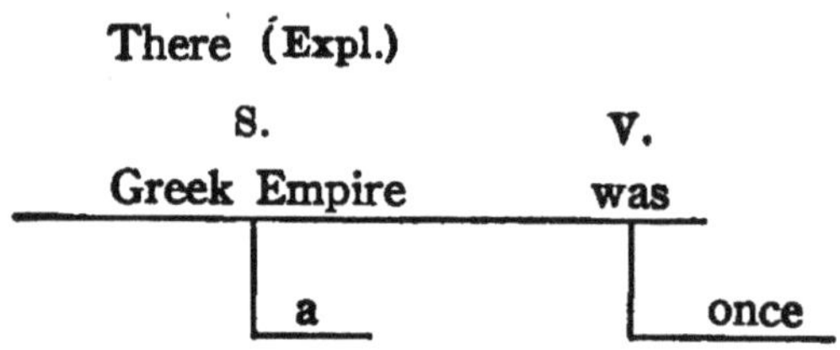

93. Phrase used substantively. [Buehler, § 56.]

Over the fence is out.

SIMPLE SENTENCE

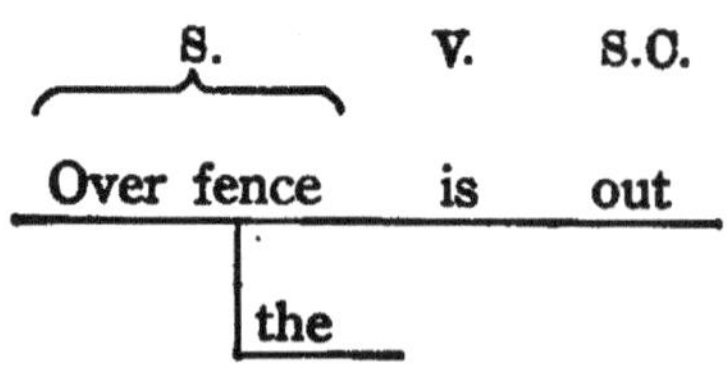

94. Correlatives "as . . . so." [Buehler, § 243.]

As a man thinketh in his heart, *so* is he.

COMPLEX SENTENCE

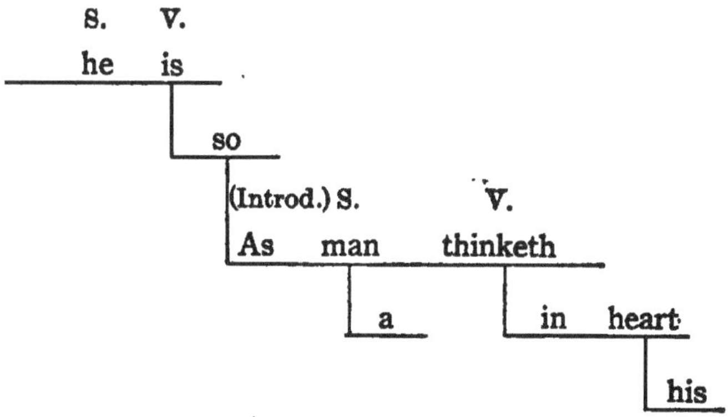

95. Sample Diagram of a long, complicated sentence.

Of man's first disobedience, and the fruit
Of that forbidden tree whose mortal taste
Brought death into the world and all our woe
With loss of Eden, till one greater Man
Restore us and regain the blissful seat,
Sing, Heavenly Muse! that on the secret top
Of Oreb or of Sinai didst inspire
That shepherd who first taught the chosen seed
In the beginning how the heavens and earth
Rose out of chaos.

Complex Sentence

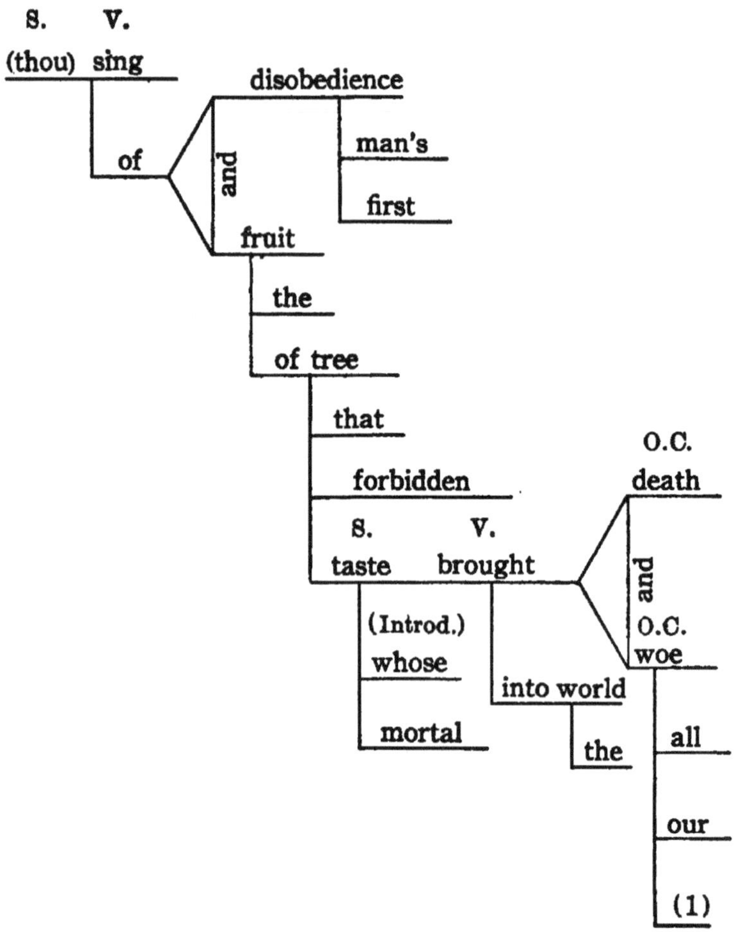

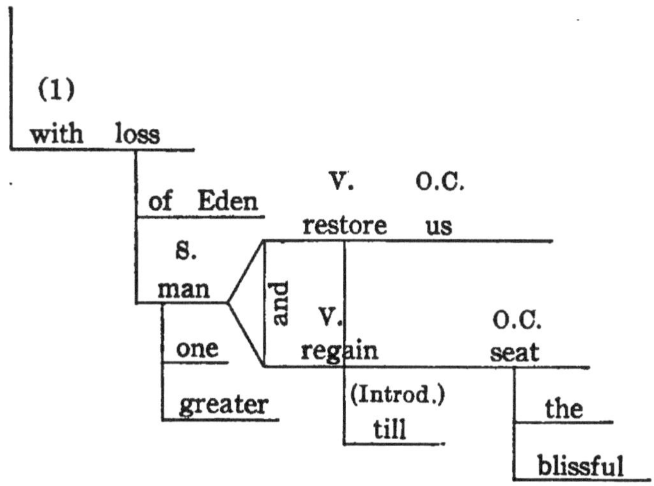
(1)
with loss
of Eden
S.
man
one
greater
and
V.
restore
O.C.
us
V.
regain
O.C.
seat
(Introd.)
till
the
blissful

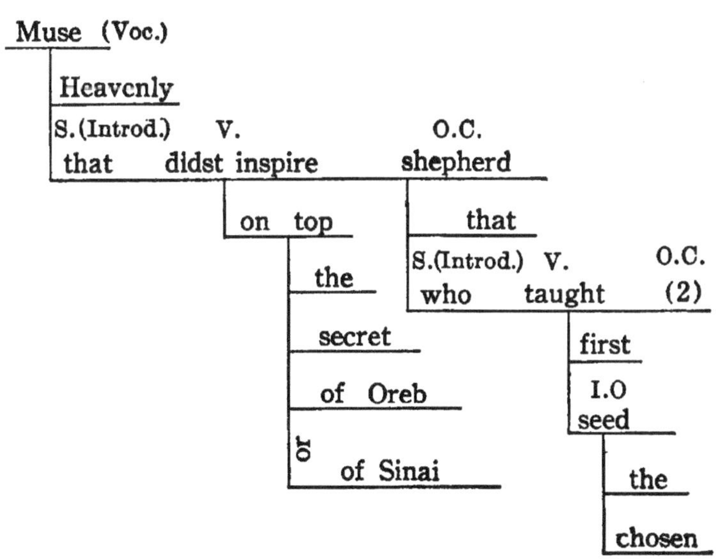
Muse (Voc.)
Heavenly
S. (Introd.)
that
V.
didst inspire
O.C.
shepherd
on top
the
secret
of Oreb
or
of Sinai
that
S.(Introd.)
who
V.
taught
O.C.
(2)
first
I.O
seed
the
chosen

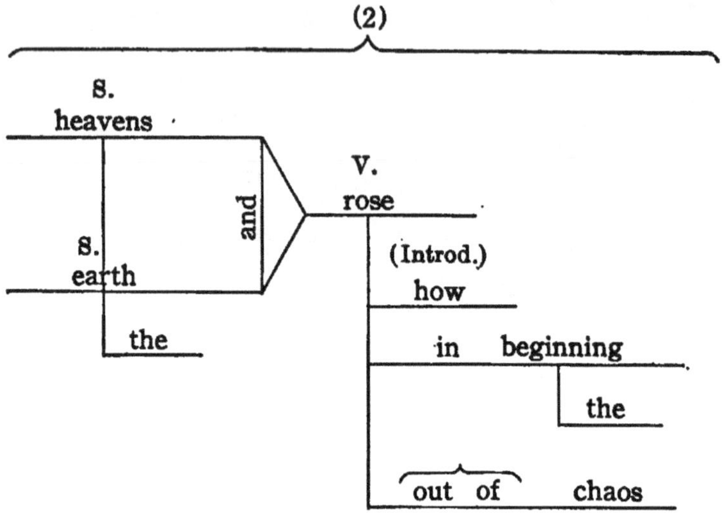
(2)
s.
heavens
s.
earth
the
and
v.
rose
(Introd.)
how
in
beginning
the
out of
chaos

EXERCISE 1

Shorter Sentences in Prose, for Diagramming

1. I suppose that very few casual readers of the *Herald* of the thirteenth of August observed, in an obscure corner, among the "Deaths," the following announcement.

2. I observed it because I was stranded at the Old Mission-House in Mackinac, waiting for a steamer which did not choose to come.

3. I was devouring, to the very stubble, all the current literature I could find.

4. My memory for names and people is good, and the reader will see that my recollection of Philip Nolan was natural enough.

5. When Aaron Burr made his first dashing expedition down the river to New Orleans, he met this gay young fellow at some dinner party.

6. Burr marked him, talked to him, walked with him, took him on a voyage in his flatboat, and fascinated him.

7. For the next year barrack-life was very tame to poor Nolan.

8. He occasionally availed himself of the permission the great man had given him, and wrote him letters.

9. Long, high-worded, stilted letters the poor boy wrote and rewrote and copied.

10. But not a line did he ever have in reply from the gay deceiver.

11. The other boys in the garrison sneered at him, because he sacrificed in this unreturned affection for a politician the time they devoted to high-low-jack.

12. But Nolan had his revenge when Burr came down the river the second time.

13. He went out in the evening on Nolan's skiff, and at the end of the sail Nolan was enlisted in body and soul.

14. From that time, though he did not yet know it, he lived as a man without a country.

15. What Burr intended I know no better than you, dear reader.

16. At the end of the trial Colonel Morgan, the judge, called upon Nolan for anything he might say in self-defense.

17. Nolan, now greatly angered, exclaimed with an oath, "I wish I may never hear of the United States again!"

18. Of course he did not know how the words shocked old Colonel Morgan.

19. Half of the officers who sat in court had served through the Revolution, and their lives had been risked for the idea which he so cavalierly cursed in his madness.

20. But Nolan had been educated on a plantation where the finest company was a Spanish officer or a French merchant from Orleans.

21. He had spent half of his youth with an elder brother hunting horses in Texas; and to him "United States" was scarcely a reality.

22. Yet he had been fed by "United States" during all his years in the army.

23. He had sworn allegiance to "United States"; "United States" had given him the uniform he wore, and the sword by his side.

24. Nay, my poor Nolan, Aaron Burr cared for you on that very account.

25. I do not excuse Nolan; I only explain to the reader the reason for his cursing his country.

26. From that moment until the day when he died, he never heard her name again.

27. Now if Nolan had compared George Washington to Benedict Arnold, Morgan would not have felt worse.

28. He called the court into his private room, and returned in fifteen minutes, with a face like a sheet.

29. Prisoner, hear the sentence of the court.

30. The court decides that you never hear the name of the United States again.

31. Nolan laughed, but nobody else laughed; old Morgan was too solemn and the whole room was hushed.

32. Then Morgan added, "Mr. Marshal, take the prisoner to Orleans in an armed boat, and deliver him to the naval commander there."

33. The marshal gave his orders, and the prisoner was taken out of court.

34. I have always supposed that Colonel Morgan himself took the proceedings of the court to Washington City, and explained them to Mr. Jefferson.

35. It is certain at least that the President approved them.

36. Before the *Nautilus* got around from New Orleans to the Atlantic Coast with the prisoner on board, the sentence had been approved, and he was a man without a country.

37. The plan then adopted was in substance that which was necessarily followed ever after.

38. Perhaps it was suggested by the necessity of sending him by water from Fort Adams to Orleans.

39. Nolan was put on a government vessel bound on a long cruise.

40. We had few long cruises then, for the navy was not in favor; and I do not know certainly what his first cruise was.

41. But the commander to whom he was intrusted regulated the etiquette and the precautions of the affair, and according to this scheme they were carried out till Nolan died.

42. When I was second officer of the *Intrepid*, I saw the original paper of instructions.

43. If I had preserved the whole of this paper, there would be no break in the beginning of my sketch of this story.

44. The rule adopted on the ships was transmitted from the beginning.

45. No mess liked to have him permanently, because his presence cut off all talk of home.

46. But we pitied his loneliness very deeply, and we finally sank into one system.

47. Talking with the men was forbidden to him unless an officer was at hand.

48. With officers he had unrestrained intercourse, but he soon grew shy.

49. Then the captain always asked him to dinner on Monday.

50. Every mess in succession took up the invitation in its turn, and according to the size of the ship, you had him at your mess more or less often at dinner.

EXERCISE 2

LONGER SENTENCES IN PROSE, FOR DIAGRAMMING

1. In a secluded and mountainous part of Styria there was, in old time, a valley of the most surprising and luxuriant fertility.

2. It was surrounded on all sides by steep and rocky mountains, rising into peaks, which were always covered with snow, and from which a number of torrents descended in constant cataracts.

3. One of these fell westward, over the face of crags so high that, when the sun had set to everything else, his beams still shone upon this waterfall, making it look like a shower of gold.

4. It was consequently called by the people of this quiet and secluded valley the Golden River.

5. It was strange that none of these streams fell into the valley itself; but all descended on the other side of the mountains, and wound away through broad plains and by populous cities.

6. But the clouds were drawn so constantly to the snowy hills, and rested so softly in the circular hollow, that, in time of drought and heat, when all the country round was burnt up, there was still rain in the little valley.

7. Its crops were heavy, its hay high, its apples red, its grapes blue, its wine rich, and its honey sweet; it was indeed a marvel to every one who beheld it, and was commonly called the Treasure Valley.

8. The whole of this little valley belonged to three brothers, Schwartz, Hans, and Gluck, of whom Schwartz

and Hans, the two elder brothers, were very ugly men, with overhanging eyebrows, and small, dull eyes, which were always half shut.

9. They lived by farming the Treasure Valley, and very good farmers they were, for they killed everything that did not pay for its eating.

10. They shot the blackbirds, because they pecked the fruit; and killed the hedgehogs, lest they should suck the cows; they poisoned the crickets for eating the crumbs in the kitchen; and smothered the cicadas, which used to sing all summer in the lime trees.

11. They worked their servants without any wages, till they would not work any more, and then quarreled with them, and turned them out of doors without paying them.

12. They generally contrived to keep their corn by them till it was very dear, and then sell it for double value; they had heaps of gold lying about on their floors, yet it was never known that they had given a penny or a crust in charity.

13. Gluck, the youngest brother, was as completely opposed, in both appearance and character, to his seniors as could possibly be imagined or desired.

14. He was not above twelve years of age, fair, blue-eyed, and kind in temper to every living thing.

15. He did not, of course, agree particularly well with brothers in whom there existed so much cruelty and selfishness.

16. They made him turn the spit, when they had any meat to roast, and that was not often; for, to do the brothers justice, they were hardly less sparing upon themselves than upon other people.

17. At other times he would clean the shoes, the floors, and the plates, getting what was left on the dishes, by way of encouragement, and a quantity of dry blows, by way of education.

18. After things had gone on in this manner for a long time, at last came a very wet summer when everything went wrong in the country round.

19. The hay had hardly been got in, when the haystacks were floated bodily down to the sea by an inundation; the vines were cut to pieces by hail; the corn was killed by a black blight; only in the Treasure Valley all was safe.

20. Everybody came to buy corn at the farm, and went away pouring maledictions on the elder brothers.

21. They asked what they liked, and got it, except from the poor people, who could only beg, and several of whom actually starved to death on their doorstep without the slightest regard or notice.

22. It was drawing toward winter, and very cold weather, when one day the two elder brothers had gone out, with their usual warning to little Gluck, who was left to mind the roast, that he must let nobody in and give nothing out.

23. Gluck sat down quite close to the fire, for it was raining very hard, and the kitchen walls were by no means dry or comfortable-looking.

24. He turned and turned the roast, until it was nice and brown, meanwhile thinking to himself, "What a pity it is that my brothers never invite anybody to dinner."

25. "I'm sure," thought he, "that when they have a piece of mutton as nice as this, some poor person should help eat it with them."

26. As he spoke, a double knock sounded at the house-door, heavy and dull, as if the knocker had been tied up, more like a puff than a knock.

27. "It must be the wind," said Gluck; "nobody else would dare to knock double knocks at our door."

28. But it was not the wind; for it came again very hard, and (what was more) the knocker seemed to be in a hurry, and not to be in the least afraid of the consequences.

29. Gluck went to the window, opened it, and put out his head to see who it was.

30. It was the most extraordinary-looking little gentleman he had ever seen in his life, a man with a very large nose, slightly brass-colored, and with cheeks that were round and red, and might have justified the guess that he had been blowing a fire for eight-and-forty hours.

31. His eyes twinkled merrily through his long silky eyelashes, while his mustaches curled twice round like a corkscrew on each side of his mouth, and his hair, of a curious pepper-and-salt color, descended far over his shoulders.

32. His doublet was prolonged behind into something resembling a violent exaggeration of what is now termed a "swallow-tail," but was much obscured by the swelling folds of an enormous black cloak.

33. This cloak must have been very much too long in calm weather, as the wind, whistling round the old house, carried it clear out from the wearer's shoulders to about four times his own length.

34. Gluck was so perfectly paralyzed by the appearance of his visitor, that he remained fixed without uttering a word, until the old gentleman, having performed another concerto on the knocker, turned round to look after his fly-away cloak.

35. In doing so he caught sight of Gluck's little yellow head jammed in the window, and cried, "That's not the way to answer the door; I'm wet; let me in."

36. To do the little gentleman justice, he was wet, indeed: his feather hung down as limply as a beaten puppy's tail, and from the ends of his mustaches the water was running in streams into his waistcoat pockets.

37. "I beg pardon, sir," said Gluck; "I'm very sorry, but I really can't let you in."

38. But Gluck, who by this time had had his head so long

out of the window that he began to feel it was really unpleasantly cold, turned and saw the beautiful fire rustling and roaring within, and took pity on the stranger.

39. He decided not only that he looked very wet, but also that it would be an act of Christian charity to let him in, if merely for a quarter of an hour.

40. Round he went to the door and opened it; and as the little gentleman walked in, through the house there came a gust of wind that made the chimneys totter.

41. Then the strange visitor walked into the kitchen, where he sat himself down on the hob, his long pointed cap sticking up the chimney, for it was too long to be accommodated within the room.

42. Although Gluck thought his guest would soon dry, he did *not* dry there, but went on dripping among the cinders, until the fire fizzed and sputtered and began to look very black and uncomfortable.

43. At length Gluck, after watching the water spread in long silver streams over the floor for almost a quarter of an hour, asked his guest whether he might not relieve him of his cloak.

44. When, however, he received a rather gruff refusal for his pains, and when, moreover, a similar offer in regard to the old gentleman's cap met with a similar reply, poor Gluck was puzzled and distressed by this odd behavior.

45. At length the old gentleman asked to be given a slice from the roast of mutton on the spit, and Gluck was forced to tell him what Hans and Schwartz would say if they found a piece of the roast gone.

46. The old gentleman nevertheless asked and asked again in so melancholy a manner that Gluck at last warmed a plate and sharpened a knife, saying to himself meanwhile that in spite of what his cruel brothers might say or do, he could not refuse to show a hungry man pity.

47. He had no sooner cut a large slice out of the mutton, than there came a tremendous rap at the door, which caused the old gentleman to jump off the hob as if it had suddenly become inconveniently warm.

48. Having hastily fitted the slice into the mutton again as well as he could in his terror, Gluck ran to open the door, for he knew it must be his brothers, and they never liked to be kept waiting, particularly in the rain.

49. It was indeed his brothers: they walked in grumbling, Schwartz throwing his umbrella in Gluck's face, and Hans administering an educational box on the ear as he followed his brother into the kitchen.

50. Imagine, if you can, the blank astonishment of both, who had not for years received a stranger into their house, when they saw, standing in the middle of the kitchen floor, the odd little gentleman Gluck had befriended, with pointed cap in hand and bowing with the utmost possible velocity.

EXERCISE 3

SHORTER SENTENCES IN POETRY, FOR DIAGRAMMING

1. Harp of the North! that moldering long hast hung
   On the witch elm that shades Saint Fillan's spring,
And down the fitful breeze thy numbers flung,
   Till envious ivy did around thee cling,
Muffling with verdant ringlet every string, —
   O Minstrel Harp, still must thine accents sleep?

2. The stag at eve had drunk his fill,
Where danced the moon on Monan's rill,
And deep his midnight lair had made
In lone Glenartney's hazel shade;
But when the sun his beacon red
Had kindled on Benvoirlich's head,
The deep-mouthed bloodhound's heavy bay
Resounded up the rocky way.

3. But ere his fleet career he took,
The dewdrops from his flanks he shook;
Like crested leader proud and high
Tossed his beamed frontlet to the sky;
A moment gazed adown the dale,
A moment snuffed the tainted gale,
A moment listened to the cry,
That thickened as the chase drew nigh;
Then, as the headmost foes appeared,
With one brave bound the copse he cleared.

4. 'Twere long to tell what steeds gave o'er
As swept the hunt through Cambusmore;
What reins were tightened in despair,
When rose Benledi's ridge in air;
Who flagged upon Bochastle's heath,
Who shunned the depth of flooded Teith —
For twice that day, from shore to shore,
The gallant stag swam stoutly o'er.

5. The Hunter marked that mountain high,
The lone lake's western boundary,
And deemed the stag must turn to bay,
Where that huge rampart barred the way;
Already glorying in the prize,
Measured his antlers with his eyes;
For the death wound and death halloo
Mustered his breath, his whinyard drew.

6. The western waves of ebbing day
Rolled o'er the glen their level way;
Each purple peak, each flinty spire,
Was bathed in floods of living fire;
But not a setting beam could glow
Within the dark ravines below,
Where twined the path in shadow hid,
Round many a rocky pyramid.

7. But scarce again his horn he wound,
When lo! forth starting at the sound,
From underneath an aged oak
That slanted from the islet rock,
A damsel guider of its way,
A little skiff shot to the bay,
That round the promontory steep
Led its deep line in graceful sweep.

8. A chieftain's daughter seemed the maid;
Her satin snood, her silken plaid,
Her golden brooch, such birth betrayed;
And seldom was a snood amid
Such wild luxuriant ringlets hid,
Whose glossy black to shame might bring
The plumage of the raven's wing.

9. It was a lodge of ample size,
But strange of structure and device;
Of such materials as around
The workman's hand had readiest found;
Lopped of their boughs, their hoar trunks bared,
And by the hatchet rudely squared,
To give the walls their destined height,
The sturdy oak and ash unite.

10. The stranger viewed the shore around;
'Twas all so close with copsewood bound,
Nor track nor pathway might declare
That human foot frequented there,
Until the mountain maiden showed
A clambering unsuspected road,
That winded through the tangled screen,
And opened on a narrow green,
Where weeping birch and willow round
With their long fibers swept the ground.

11. For while he lingered there,
A doubt that ever smoldered in the hearts
Of those great lords and barons of his realm
Flashed forth and into war; for most of these,
Colleaguing with a score of petty kings,
Made head against him, crying: "Who is he?"

12. And Arthur, passing thence to battle, felt
Travail, and throes and agonies of the life,
Desiring that he be joined with Guinevere,
And thinking as he rode: "Her father said
That there between the man and beast they die;
Shall I not lift her from this land of beasts?"

13. That story which the bold Sir Bedivere,
First made and latest left of all the knights,
Told, when the man was no more than a voice
In the white winter of his age, to those
With whom he dwelt, new faces, other minds.

14. The mother's eye,
Full of the wistful fear that he would go,
And turning toward him whensoever he turned,
Perplexed his outward purpose, till an hour
When, wakened by the wind which with full voice
Swept bellowing through the darkness on to dawn,
He rose, and out of slumber calling two
That still had tended on him from his birth,
Before the wakeful mother heard him, went.

15. Then into hall Gareth ascending heard
A voice, the voice of Arthur, and beheld
Far over heads in that long-vaulted hall
The splendor of the presence of the King,
Throned, and delivering doom — and looked no more —
But felt his young heart hammering in his ears,
And thought, "For this half-shadow of a lie
The truthful King will doom me when I speak."

16. He therefore turning softly like a thief,
Lest the harsh shingle should grate under foot,

And feeling all along the garden wall,
Lest he should swoon and tumble and be found,
Crept to the gate, and opened it and closed,
As lightly as a sick man's chamber door,
Behind him, and came out upon the waste.

17. Downward from his mountain gorge
Stepped the long-haired, long-bearded solitary,
Brown, looking hardly human, strangely clad,
Muttering and mumbling, idiot like, it seemed,
With inarticulate rage, and making signs
They knew not what; and yet he led the way
To where the rivulets of sweet water ran.

18. And ever as he mingled with the crew,
And heard them talking, his long bounden tongue
Was loosened, till he made them understand;
Whom, when their casks were filled, they took aboard;
And there the tale he uttered brokenly,
Scarce credited at first, but more and more,
Amazed and melted all who listened to it.

19. Their names, their years, spelt by the unlettered Muse,
The place of fame and elegy supply;
And many a holy text around she strews,
That teach the rustic moralist to die;
For who, to dumb forgetfulness a prey,
This pleasing anxious being e'er resigned,
Left the warm precincts of the cheerful day,
Nor cast one longing lingering look behind?

20. So said he, and the barge with oar and sail
Moved from the brink, like some full-breasted swan
That, fluting a wild carol ere her death,

Ruffles her pure cold plume, and takes the flood
With swarthy webs; long stood Sir Bedivere
Revolving many memories, till the hull
Looked one black dot against the verge of dawn,
And on the mere the wailing died away.

21. Then rose Elaine and glided through the fields,
And passed beneath the weirdly sculptured gates
Far up the dim rich city to her kin;
There bode the night, but woke with dawn, and passed
Down through the dim rich city to the fields;
So day by day she passed
In either twilight ghost-like to and fro
Gliding.

22. Then if the maiden, while that ghostly grace
Beamed on his fancy, spoke, he answered not,
Or short and coldly, and she knew right well
What the rough sickness meant, but what this meant
She knew not, and the sorrow dimmed her sight,
And drove her ere her time across the fields
Far into the rich city, where alone
She murmured, "Vain, in vain! it cannot be."

23. Gawain the while through all the region round
Rode with his diamond, wearied of the quest,
Touched at all points except the poplar grove,
And came at last, though late, to Astolat;
Whom glittering in enamelled arms the maid
Glanced at, and cried, "What news from Camelot, lord?"

24. So for long hours sat Enid by her lord
There in the naked hall, propping his head,

And chafing his pale hands, and calling to him,
Till at the last he wakened from his swoon,
And found his own dear bride propping his head,
And chafing his faint hands, and calling to him;
And felt the warm tears falling on his face.

25. So through the green gloom of the wood they passed,
And issuing under open heavens beheld
A little town with towers, upon a rock,
And close beneath, a meadow gemlike chased
In the brown wild, and mowers mowing in it;
And down a rocky pathway from the place
There came a fair-haired youth, that in his hand
Bare victual for the mowers.

26. So Gareth all for glory underwent
The sooty yoke of kitchen vassalage,
Ate with young lads his portion by the door,
And couched at night with grimy kitchen-knaves;
And Lancelot ever spake him pleasantly,
But Kay, the seneschal, who loved him not,
Would hustle and harry him, and labor him
Beyond his comrades of the hearth.

EXERCISE 4

LONGER SENTENCES IN POETRY, FOR DIAGRAMMING

1. And even in saying this,
Her memory from old habit of the mind
Went slipping back upon the golden days
In which she saw him first, when Lancelot came,
Reputed the best knight and goodliest man,
Ambassador, to yield her to his lord
Arthur, and led her forth, and far ahead
Of his and her retinue moving, they,
Rapt in sweet talk or lively, all on love
And sports and tilts and pleasure,
Rode under groves that looked a paradise
Of blossom.

2. But I was first of all the kings who drew
The knighthood-errant of this realm and all
The realms together under me, their Head,
In that fair Order of my Table Round,
A glorious company, the flower of men,
To serve as model for the mighty world,
And be the fair beginning of a time.

3. O me! for why is all around us here
As if some lesser god had made the world,
But had not force to shape it as he would,
Till the High God behold it from beyond,
And enter it, and make it beautiful?

Or else as if the world were wholly fair,
But that these eyes of men are dense and dim,
And have not power to see it as it is?

4. Then, ere that last weird battle in the west,
There came on Arthur sleeping, Gawain killed
In Lancelot's war, the ghost of Gawain blown
Along a wandering wind, and past his ear
Went shrilling: "Hollow, hollow all delight!
Hail, King! to-morrow thou shalt pass away;
Farewell! there is an isle of rest for thee."

5. And fainter onward, like wild birds that change
Their season in the night and wail their way
From cloud to cloud, down the long wind the dream
Shrilled; but in going mingled with dim cries
Far in the moonlit haze among the hills,
As of some lonely city sacked by night,
When all is lost, and wife and child with wail
Pass to new lords.

6. Nor ever yet had Arthur fought a fight
Like this last, dim, weird battle of the west;
A death-white mist slept over sand and sea,
Whereof the chill, to him who breathed it, drew
Down with his blood, till all his heart was cold
With formless fear; and even on Arthur fell
Confusion, since he saw not whom he fought;
For friend and foe were shadows in the mist,
And friend slew friend not knowing whom he slew.

7. So all day long the noise of battle rolled
Among the mountains by the winter sea,
Until King Arthur's Table, man by man,

Had fallen in Lyonesse about their lord,
King Arthur; then, because his wound was deep,
The bold Sir Bedivere uplifted him,
And bore him to a chapel nigh the field,
That stood on a dark strait of barren land.

8. I think that we
Shall never more, at any future time,
Delight our souls with talk of knightly deeds,
Walking about the gardens and the halls
Of Camelot, as in the days that were;
I perish by this people which I made —
Though Merlin sware that I should come again
To rule once more — but let what will be be;
I am so deeply smitten through the helm
That without help I cannot last till morn.

9. And Gareth answered her with kindling eyes:
"Gold? said I gold? — ay then, why he, or she,
Or whosoe'er it was, or half the world
Had ventured — had the thing I spake of been
Mere gold — but this was all of that true steel
Whereof they forged the brand Excalibur,
And lightnings played about it in the storm,
And all the little fowl were flurried at it,
And there were cries and clashings in the nest."

10. So when the Queen, who long had sought in vain
To break him from the intent to which he grew,
Found her son's will unwaveringly one,
She answered craftily: "Will you walk through fire?
Who walks through fire will hardly heed the smoke;
Ay, go then, if you must; only one proof,
Before thou ask the King to make thee knight,

Of thine obedience and thy love to me,
Thy mother, — I demand."

11. So till the dusk that followed evensong
Rode on the two, reviler and reviled;
Then after one long slope was mounted, saw,
Bowl shaped, through tops of many thousand pines
A gloomy-gladed hollow slowly sink
To westward — in the deeps of which a mere,
Round as the red eye of an eagle-owl,
Under the half dead sunset glared; and shouts
Ascended, and there break a serving-man
Flying from out of the black wood, and crying,
"They have bound my lord to cast him in the mere!"

12. Meanwhile the new companions passed away
Far o'er the long backs of the bushless downs,
To where Sir Lancelot knew there lived a knight
Not far from Camelot, now for forty years
A hermit, who had prayed, labor'd and prayed,
And ever laboring had scooped himself
In the white rock a chapel and a hall
On massive columns, like a shore-cliff cave,
And cells and chambers.

13. But when the next day broke from underground,
And shot red fire and shadows through the cave,
They rose, heard mass, broke fast, and rode away;
Then Lancelot saying, "Hear, but hold my name
Hidden, you ride with Lancelot of the Lake,"
Abashed Lavaine, whose instant reverence,
Dearer to true young hearts than their own praise,
But left him leave to stammer.

14. Last, as by some one death-bed after wail
Of suffering, silence follows, or through death
Or death-like swoon, thus over all that shore,
Save for some whisper of the seething seas,
A dead hush fell; but when the dolorous day
Grew drearier toward twilight falling, came
A bitter wind, clear from the north, and blew
The mist aside, and with that wind the tide
Rose, and the pale King glanced across the field
Of battle.

15. And Merlin looked and half believed her true,
So tender was her voice, so fair her face,
So sweetly gleamed her eyes behind her tears
Like sunlight on the plain behind a shower;
And yet he answered half indignantly:
"Far other was the song that once I heard
By this huge oak, sung nearly where we sit;
For here we met, some ten or twelve of us,
To chase a creature that was current then
In these wild woods, the hart with golden horns."

16. She hated all the knights, and heard in thought
Their lavish comment when her name was named;
For once, when Arthur, walking all alone,
Vext at a rumor issued from herself
Of some corruption crept among his knights,
Had met her, Vivien, being greeted fair,
Would fain have wrought upon his cloudy mood
With reverent eyes mock-loyal, shaken voice,
And fluttered adoration, and at last
With dark sweet hints of some who prized him more
Than who should prize him most; at which the King
Had gazed upon her blankly and gone by.

17. It made the laughter of an afternoon
That Vivien should attempt the blameless king;
And after that, she set herself to gain
Him, the most famous man of all those times,
Merlin, who knew the range of all their arts,
Had built the King his havens, ships, and halls,
Was also bard, and knew the starry heavens;
The people called him wizard; whom at first
She played about with slight and sprightly talk,
And vivid smiles, and faintly-venomed points
Of slander, glancing here and grazing there;
And yielding to his kindlier moods, the seer
Would watch her at her petulance and play,
Even when they seemed unlovable, and laugh
As those that watch a kitten.

18. Thus he grew
Tolerant of what he half disdained, and she,
Perceiving that she was but half disdained,
Began to break her sports with graver fits,
Turn red or pale, would often when they met
Sigh fully, or all silent gaze upon him
With such a fixt devotion that the old man,
Though doubtful, felt the flattery, and at times
Would flatter his own wish in age for love,
And half believe her true.

19. Thus, as a hearth lit in a mountain home,
And glancing on the window, when the gloom
Of twilight deepens round it, seems a flame
That rages in the woodland far below,
So when his moods were darkened, court and king
And all the kindly warmth of Arthur's hall
Shadowed an angry distance; yet he strove

To learn the graces of their Table, fought
Hard with himself, and seemed at length in peace.

20. Then chanced, one morning, that Sir Balin sat
Close-bowered in that garden nigh the hall;
A walk of roses ran from door to door,
A walk of lilies crossed it to the bower;
And down that range of roses the great Queen
Came with slow steps, the morning on her face;
And all in shadow from the counter door
Sir Lancelot as to meet her, then at once,
As if he saw not, glanced aside, and paced
The long white walk of lilies toward the bower.

21. None of these
Came from his country, or could answer him,
If questioned, aught of what he cared to know;
And dull the voyage was with long delays,
The vessel scarce sea-worthy; but evermore
His fancy fled before the lazy wind
Returning, till beneath a clouded moon
He like a lover down through all his blood
Drew in the dewy meadowy morning-breath
Of England, blown across her ghostly wall.

22. Then down the long street having slowly stolen,
His heart foreshadowing all calamity,
His eyes upon the stones, he reached the home
Where Annie lived and loved him, and his babes
In those far-off seven happy years were born;
But finding neither light nor murmur there —
A bill of sale gleamed through the drizzle — crept
Still downward, thinking, "dead, or dead to me!"

23. And Vivien, like the tenderest-hearted maid
That ever bided tryst at village stile,
Made answer, either eyelid wet with tears:
"Nay, Master, be not wrathful with your maid;
Caress her, let her feel herself forgiven
Who feels no heart to ask another boon;
I think ye hardly know the tender rime
Of 'trust me not at all or all in all;'
I heard the great Sir Lancelot sing it once,
And it shall answer for me."

24. And Lancelot answered nothing, but he went,
And at the inrunning of a little brook
Sat by the river in a cove, and watched
The high reed wave, and lifted up his eyes
And saw the barge that brought her moving down,
Far off, a blot upon the stream, and said
Low in himself: "Ah, simple heart and sweet,
Ye loved me, damsel, surely with a love
Far tenderer than my Queen's; pray for thy soul?
Ay, that will I; farewell too — now at last —
Farewell, fair lily."

25. Down to the pool and narrow wharf he went,
Seeking a tavern which of old he knew,
A front of timber-crost antiquity,
So propped, worm-eaten, ruinously old,
He thought it must have gone; but he was gone
Who kept it, and his widow, Miriam Lane,
With daily-dwindling profits held the house,
A haunt of brawling seamen once, but now
Stiller, with yet a bed for wandering men;
There Enoch rested silent many days.

26. Here both were mute, till Philip glancing up
Beheld the dead flame of the falling day
Pass from the Danish barrow overhead;
Then, fearing night and chill for Annie, rose
And sent his voice beneath him through the wood;
Up came the children laden with their spoil;
Then all descended to the port, and there
At Annie's door he paused and gave his hand,
Saying gently, "Annie, when I spoke to you,
That was your hour of weakness."

EXERCISE 5

DIFFICULT SENTENCES IN POETRY, FOR DIAGRAMMING

1. I read, before my eyelids dropped their shade,
   "The Legend of Good Women," long ago
   Sung by the morning star of song, who made
   His music heard below,
   Dan Chaucer, the first warbler, whose sweet breath
   Preluded those melodious bursts, that fill
   The spacious times of great Elizabeth
   With sounds that echo still;
   And, for a while, the knowledge of his art
   Held me above the subject, as strong gales
   Hold swollen clouds from raining, though my heart,
   Brimful of those wild tales,
   Charged both mine eyes with tears; in every land
   I saw, wherever light illumineth,
   Beauty and anguish walking hand in hand
   The downward slope to death.

2. Morn in the white wake of the morning star
   Came furrowing all the orient into gold;
   We rose, and, each by other dressed with care,
   Descended to the court that lay three parts
   In shadow, but the Muses' heads were touched
   Above the darkness from their native east;
   There while we stood beside the fount, and watched
   Or seemed to watch the dancing bubble, approached
   Melissa, tinged with wan from lack of sleep.

3. Warrior of God, whose strong right arm debased
The throne of Persia, when her Satrap bled
At Issus by the Syrian gates, or fled
Beyond the Memnian naphtha pits, disgraced
For ever — thee — thy pathway sand erased —
Gliding with equal crowns two serpents led
Joyful to that palm-planted fountain-fed
Ammonian Oasis in the waste;
There in a silent shade of laurel brown
Apart the Chamian Oracle divine
Sheltered his unapproached mysteries.

4. Thenceforward oft from out a despot dream
The father panting woke, and oft, as dawn
Aroused the black republic on his elms,
Sweeping the froth-fly from the fescue, brushed
Through the dim meadow toward his treasure trove,
Seized it, took home, and to my lady — who made
A downward crescent of her minion mouth,
Listless in all despondence, — read, and tore
As if the living passion symbolled there
Were living nerves to feel the rent; and burnt
Now chafing at his own great self defied,
Now striking on huge stumbling-blocks of scorn
In babyisms and dear diminutives
Scattered all over the vocabulary
Of such a love as like a chidden child,
After much wailing, hushed itself at last
Hopeless of answer.

5. Then rose the king and moved his host by night,
And ever pushed Sir Modred league by league,
Back to the sunset bound of Lyonesse,
A land of old upheaven from the abyss

By fire, to sink into the abyss again;
Where fragments of forgotten peoples dwelt,
And the long mountains ended in a coast
Of ever shifting sand, and far away
The phantom circle of a moaning sea;
There the pursuer could pursue no more,
And he that fled no further fly the king;
And there, that day when the great light of heaven
Burned at his lowest in the rolling year,
On the waste sand by the waste sea they closed.

6. Yet pressing on, though all in fear, to find
Sir Gawain or Sir Modred, he saw nor one
Nor other, but in all the listening eyes
Of those tall knights, that ranged about the throne,
Clear honor shining like the dewy star
Of dawn, and faith in their great king, with pure
Affection, and the light of victory,
And glory gained, and ever more to gain.

7. As a huge stone is sometimes seen to lie
Couched on the bald top of an eminence,
Wonder to all who do the same espy,
By what means it could thither come, and whence;
So that it seems a thing endued with sense:
Like a Sea-beast crawled forth, that on a shelf
Of rock or sand reposeth, there to sun itself;
Such seemed this man, not all alive nor dead,
Nor all asleep — in his extreme old age;
His body was bent double, feet and head
Coming together in life's pilgrimage;
As if some dire constraint of pain, or rage
Of sickness felt by him in times long passed,
A more than human weight upon his frame had cast.

8. It is not to be thought of, that the flood
Of British freedom, which to the open sea
Of the world's praise from dark antiquity
Hath flowed, "with pomp of waters, unwithstood,"
Roused though it be full often to a mood
Which spurns the check of salutary bands,
That this most famous stream in bogs and sands
Should perish, and to evil and to good
Be lost forever; in our Halls is hung
Armory of the invincible Knights of old;
We must be free or die, who speak the tongue
That Shakespeare spake, the faith and morals hold
Which Milton held.

9. If I were loved as I desire to be,
What is there in the great sphere of the earth,
And range of evil between death and birth,
That I should fear, if I were loved by thee? —
All the inner, all the outer world of pain
Clear love would pierce and cleave, if thou wert mine,
As I have heard that, somewhere in the main,
Fresh water springs come up through bitter brine;
'Twere joy, not fear, clasped hand in hand with thee,
To wait for death.

10. I stand beneath the tree, whose branches shade
Thy western window, Chapel of St. John!
And hear its leaves repeat their benison
On him, whose hand thy stones memorial laid;
Then I remember one of whom was said
In the world's darkest hour, "Behold thy son!"
And see him living still, and wandering on
And waiting for the advent long delayed.

11\. Poet! I come to touch thy lance with mine;
Not as a knight, who on the listed field
Of tourney touched his adversary's shield
In token of defiance, but in sign
Of homage to the mastery, which is thine,
In English song; nor will I keep concealed,
And voiceless as a rivulet frost-congealed,
My admiration for thy verse divine;
Not of the howling dervishes of song,
Who craze the brain with their delirious dance,
Art thou, O sweet historian of the heart!
Therefore to thee the laurel leaves belong.

12\. As one who, walking in the twilight gloom,
  Hears round about him voices as it darkens,
And seeing not the forms from which they come,
  Pauses from time to time, and turns and hearkens;
So walking here in twilight, O my friends!
  I hear your voices, softened by the distance,
And pause, and turn to listen, as each sends
  His words of friendship, comfort and assistance;
If any thought of mine, or sung or told,
  Has ever given delight or consolation,
Ye have repaid me back a thousand fold,
  By every friendly sign and salutation.

13\. I, writing thus, am still what men call young;
I have not so far left the coasts of life
To travel inland, that I cannot hear
That murmur of the outer Infinite
Which unweaned babies smile at in their sleep
When wondered at for smiling; not so far,
But still I catch my mother at her post
Beside the nursery door, with finger up,

"Hush, hush, here's too much noise!" while her sweet eyes
Leap forward, taking part against her word
In the child's riot.

14. If her kiss
Had left a longer weight upon my lips,
It might have steadied the uneasy breath,
And reconciled and fraternized my soul
With the new order;
I felt a mother-want about the world,
And still went seeking, like a bleating lamb
Left out at night in shutting up the fold, —
As restless as a nest-deserted bird,
Grown chill through something's being away, though what
It knows not; I, Aurora Leigh, was born
To make my father sadder, and myself
Not overjoyous, truly.

15. Faint as a climate-changing bird that flies
All night across the darkness, and at dawn
Falls on the threshold of her native land,
And can no more, thou camest, O my child,
Led upward by the God of ghosts and dreams,
Who laid thee at Eleusis, dazed and dumb
With passing through at once from state to state,
Until I brought thee hither, that the day,
When here thy hands let fall the gathered flower,
Might break through clouded memories once again
On thy lost self.

16. A sudden nightingale
Saw thee, and flashed into a frolic of song
And welcome; and a gleam as of the moon,
When first she peers along the tremulous deep,
Fled wavering o'er thy face, and chased away
That shadow of a likeness to the king
Of shadows, thy dark mate; thine eyes
Again were human — godlike; and the sun
Burst from a swimming fleece of winter gray,
And robed thee in his day from head to feet.

17. So said my father — and that night the bard
Sang Arthur's glorious wars, and sang the King
As wellnigh more than man, and railed at those
Who called him the false son of Gorloïs;
For there was no man knew from whence he came;
But after tempest, when the long wave broke
All down the thundering shores of Bude and Bos,
There came a day as still as heaven, and then
They found a naked child upon the sands
Of dark Tintagil by the Cornish sea,
And that was Arthur, and they fostered him
Till he by miracle was approven King;
And his grave would be a mystery
From all men, like his birth; and could he find
A woman in her womanhood as great
As he was in his manhood, then, he sang,
The twain together well might change the world.

18. But as a man to whom a dreadful loss
Falls in a far land and he knows it not,
But coming back he learns it, and the loss
So pains him that he sickens nigh to death;

So fared it with Geraint, who, being pricked
In combat with the followers of Limours,
Bled underneath his armor secretly,
And so rode on, nor told his gentle wife
What ailed him, hardly knowing it himself,
Till his eye darkened and his helmet wagged;
And at a sudden swerving of the road,
Though happily down on a bank of grass,
The prince, without a word, from his horse fell.

19. As when we dwell upon a word we know,
Repeating, till the word we know so well
Becomes a wonder, and we know not why,
So dwelt the father on her face, and thought,
"Is this Elaine?" till back the maiden fell,
Then gave a languid hand to each, and lay,
Speaking a still good-morrow with her eyes;
At last she said: "Sweet brothers, yesternight
I seemed a curious little maid again,
As happy as when we dwelt among the woods,
And when ye used to take me with the flood
Up the great river in the boatman's boat."

20. But when the morning of a tournament,
By these in earnest, those in mockery, called
The Tournament of the Dead Innocence,
Brake with a wet wind blowing, Lancelot,
Round whose sick head all night, like birds of prey,
The words of Arthur flying shrieked, arose,
And down a street-way hung with folds of pure
White samite, and by fountains running wine,
Where children sat in white with cups of gold,
Moved to the lists, and there, with slow sad steps
Ascending, filled his double-dragoned chair.

21. So dame and damsel glittered at the feast
Variously gay; for he that tells the tale
Likened them, saying, as when an hour of cold
Falls on the mountain in midsummer snows,
And all the purple slopes of mountain flowers
Pass under white, till the warm hour returns
With veer of wind and all are flowers again,
So dame and damsel cast the simple white,
And glowing in all colors, the live grass,
Rose-campion, bluebell, kingcup, poppy, glanced
About the revels and, with mirth so loud
Beyond all use, that, half amazed, the Queen,
And wroth at Tristram, and the lawless jousts,
Brake up their sports, then slowly to her bower
Parted, and in her bosom pain was lord.

22. Sadly as some old medieval knight
Gazed at the arms he could no longer wield,
The sword two-handed and the shining shield
Suspended in the hall, and full in sight,
While secret longings for the lost delight
Of tourney or adventure in the field
Came over him, and tears but half concealed
Trembled and fell upon his beard of white,
So I behold these books upon their shelf,
My ornaments and arms of other days;
Not wholly useless, though no longer used,
For they remind me of my other self.

23. Even to the last dip of the vanishing sail
She watched it, and departed weeping for him;
Then, though she mourned his absence as his grave,
Set her sad will no less to chime with his,

But throve not in her trade, not being bred
To barter, nor compensating the want
By shrewdness, neither capable of lies,
Nor asking overmuch and taking less,
And still foreboding, "What would Enoch say?"
For more than once, in days of difficulty
And pressure, had she sold her wares for less
Than what she gave in buying what she sold.

24. White swan of cities, slumbering in thy nest
So wonderfully built among the reeds
Of the lagoon, that fences thee and feeds,
As sayeth thy old historian and thy guest!
White water lily, cradled and caressed
By ocean streams, and from the silt and weeds
Lifting thy golden filaments and seeds,
Thy sun illumined spires, thy crown and crest!
White phantom city, whose untrodden streets
Are rivers, and whose pavements are the shifting
Shadows of palaces and strips of sky!
I wait to see thee vanish like the fleets
Seen in mirage.

25. And if I said that Fancy, led by Love,
Would play with flying forms and images,
Yet this is also true, that, long before
I looked upon her, when I heard her name
My heart was like a prophet to my head,
And told me I should love; a crowd of hopes,
That sought to sow themselves like winged seeds,
Born out of everything I heard and saw,
Fluttered about my senses and my soul;
And vague desires, like fitful blasts of balm

To one that travels quickly, made the air
Of life delicious, and all kinds of thought,
That verged upon them, sweeter than the dream
Dreamed by a happy man, when the dark East,
Unseen, is brightening to his bridal morn.

26. The Dragon's cave
Half hid, they tell me, now in flowing vines —
Where once he dwelt and whence he rolled himself
At dead of night — thou knowest, and that smooth rock
Before it, altar-fashioned, where of late
The woman-breasted Sphinx, with wings drawn back,
Folded her lion paws, and looked on Thebes;
There blanch the bones of whom she slew, and these
Mixed with her own, because the fierce beast found
A wiser than herself, and dashed herself
Dead in her rage.

27. Fairer thy fate than mine, if life's best end
Be to end well; and thou refusing this,
Unvenerable will thy memory be
While men shall move the lips; but if thou dare —
Thou, one of these, the race of Cadmus — then
No stone is fitted in yon marble girth
Whose echo shall not tongue thy glorious doom,
Nor in this pavement but shall ring thy name
To every hoof that clangs it, and the springs
Of Dirce laving yonder battle plain,
Heard from the roofs by night, will murmur thee
To thine own Thebes, while Thebes through thee shall stand
Firm-based with all her Gods.

28. These eyeless eyes, that cannot see thine own,
See this, that only in thy virtue lies
The saving of thy Thebes; for, yesternight,
To me, the great god Ares, whose one bliss
Is war and human sacrifice — himself
Blood-red from battle, spear and helmet tipped
With stormy light as on a mast at sea,
Stood out before a darkness, crying, "Thebes,
Thy Thebes shall fall and perish, for I loathe
The seed of Cadmus;" my son,
No sound is breathed so potent to coerce,
And to conciliate, as their names who dare
For that sweet motherland which gave them birth
Nobly to do, nobly to die.

29. Seven days I drove along the dreary deep,
And with me drove the moon and all the stars;
And the wind fell, and on the seventh night
I heard the shingle grinding in the surge,
And felt the boat shock earth, and looking up,
Beheld the enchanted towers of Carbonek,
A castle like a rock upon a rock,
With chasm-like portals open to the sea,
And steps that met the breaker; there was none
Stood near it but a lion on each side
That kept the entry, and the moon was full.

30. Then, on a golden autumn eventide,
The younger people making holiday,
With bag and sack and basket, great and small
Went nutting to the hazels; Philip stayed,
His father lying sick and needing him,
An hour behind; but as he climbed the hill,

Just where the prone edge of the wood began
To feather toward the hollow, saw the pair,
Enoch and Annie, sitting hand in hand,
His large gray eyes and weather-beaten face
All kindled by a still and sacred fire,
That burned as on an altar.

PARSING SCHEME

THE following method of parsing is suggested; if strictly adhered to, it will ensure uniform, neat, and accurate work.

In parsing, observe always the following directions. By means of two lines drawn lengthwise down your paper, divide the space into three columns, making the third column considerably the widest. In the first column write the word to be parsed; in the second, its part of speech; and in the third, all the details. The details to be given, and the order in which they are to be given, are as follows. Both the details and the order must be learned by heart.

Noun	Construction Case Number Gender Class
Pronoun	Construction Case Antecedent (*if any*) Person Number Gender Class
Adjective	Construction Comparison Class
Adverb	Construction Comparison Class (*according to use*)

Verb	Construction Person Number Tense Mode Voice Transitive or intransitive Principal parts
Infinitive	Construction Tense Voice Transitive or intransitive Principal parts
Participle	Construction Tense Voice Transitive or intransitive Principal parts
Preposition	Construction (*the phrase it introduces, and the construction of the phrase*).
Conjunction	Construction (*if coördinating, what it connects; if subordinating, the clause it introduces, and the construction of the clause*). Class
Interjection	No construction

GRAMMAR REFERENCES

FOLLOWING is a list of the sections in Buehler's *A Modern English Grammar Revised* (Newson and Company, New York) which are referred to in this Handbook, with the numbers of the corresponding Model Sentences.

21 : 1.
27 : 1.
38 : 3, 11.
39 : 1.
40 : 4, 12.
43 ff. : 7, 13–15, 74, 75, 87, 88.
49 : 18–27, 35–37.
52 : 6.
53 : 5, 23.
54 : 8.
56 : 93.
58 : 38.
59 : 39, 42.
60 : 40.
62 : 80.
64 : 81.
66 : 83.
68 : 82.
70 : 30–33.
71 : 35–40.
73 : 34, 41.
78 : 50–55, 85.
82 : 10.
85 : 13–15.
86 : 9.
87 : 28.
93 : 65–68, 70–73.
94 : 56–64, 71–73.
114 : 80, 84, 85.
115 : 79.
116 : 7.
120 : 86.
131 : 91.
133 : 7.
143 : 46, 47.
144 ff. : 18–27.
147 : 27.
150 : 89, 90.
151 : 54.
153 : 26.
167 : 11.
171 : 43, 46, 47.
176 : 92.
178 : 79.
188 : 2, 20.
222 : 65–68, 70.
223 : 84, 85.
229 : 56–64.
230 : 69.
239 : 16, 17.
242 : 28, 43, 44, 48.
243 : 48, 94.

INDEX

to the constructions, terms, parts of speech, and special words, illustrated in the Model Sentences. The Model Sentences are referred to by number.

CPSIA information can be obtained
at www.ICGtesting.com
Printed in the USA
BVHW03s0213090518
515722BV00006B/102/P

9 781375 708371